INTRODUCTION

What this book's really about

This book contains everything you need to become a great presenter. But I'm going to let you into a secret: this book isn't *really* about presenting. It's about you.

Let me make some guesses about you: you need help with your presenting – quickly. You need help because you're *busy* – and you're getting busier.

You've probably presented a bit, maybe even a lot, but you're unsatisfied with what you've done so far, and you know that you could be much better at it *if only you had more time.*

Perhaps you have one of the following needs:

- Presenting is becoming an increasingly important part of your role. You need to give clear, credible presentations, often with little preparation time.

- Client presentations and winning new business

are crucial to your organisation. You need to deliver compelling presentations that outshine the competition.

- You've reached a new level in your career, and you're having to go beyond your comfort zone in presenting. This might mean larger audiences, or more senior ones. Maybe you even have to ditch the PowerPoint and speak more off the cuff.

You know that, with the right approach, you could be less nervous. You could have better, more structured messages and create presentations that really excite and interest people. You know that you'd get more buy-in for your ideas and expand your professional reputation.

At the moment, you likely feel that presenting is something to be endured. Perhaps you think that you're just getting by, but deep down you know that if you could be better at it then lots of other opportunities would open up for you. You've probably seen this happen for colleagues and friends.

You've almost certainly seen some great presenters and wondered how they do it – how do they seem so likeable so quickly? How do they make their messages stick? Why do their audiences seem so engaged and enthusiastic during, and after, their presentations? What is that magic formula that distinguishes a great presenter from a mediocre one?

You've probably also started to realise (and if you haven't already, you will by the end of this book) that presenting is not just a luxury in your professional life.

THE BUSY PERSON'S GUIDE TO
GREAT
PRESENTING

Become a compelling, confident presenter. Every time.

LEE WARREN

RƎTHINK PRESS

First published in Great Britain 2018
by Rethink Press (www.rethinkpress.com)

Contents

Introduction   **1**

   What this book's really about   1

   How this book will save you time   3

   Why is this book different?   5

   Why you should present more   7

   Why all presentations are selling something   13

   The MAP process   15

One The Message   **21**

   The importance of the message   21

   How to find your message with a single
   question   23

   How to structure your message and make it
   flow   35

   Hook the audience   38

   An intriguing, provocative, or rhetorical
   question   41

   A quotation or inspirational comment   44

   An unusual fact   48

A funny thing happened on the way here…   50

A picture paints…   52

Slides and props   53

The Rule of Three   55

Three thirds   60

Story/Anecdote   63

Data   70

Something for the audience   75

Layering the presentation   77

Summary   79

Always have a punchline   81

Repeat, repeat, repeat   88

How a ham pie can make your message
persuasive   91

Two   The Audience   101

Nobody is interested in you   101

How to get into your audiences' heads   103

Don't tell them what they want to hear   110

Everyone you present to is tired, hungover, or
late   111

How to customise for difference audiences   112

Peaks and troughs   118

How to prepare for difficult audiences   121

The audience checklist   127

Three   The Presenter   129

I'm so nervous!   130

The one-minute warm-up   132

Rehearsal, practice, and the important
difference   137

How to sound confident 142

The eyes have it 147

What do I do with my hands? 150

Move the body 154

Notes and props 157

You're joking! 161

Any questions? 164

Deadly distractions 169

Four   The Busy Person's Guide To Slides **173**

Do without 173

Use an expert 175

Do it yourself 179

Slides or hand-outs? 184

Dealing with slide decks 187

Five   The Not-so Busy Presenter **191**

Presenting in teams 191

Mind your language 202

The Big Client 206

Online presentations 209

How to ask for feedback 213

Ideal introductions 215

Afterword **219**

Acknowledgements **223**

The Author **225**

It's an essential skill, and being known as a good presenter is one of the best ways to open up opportunities in every area of your professional life.

You know that if you could present well you'd connect better with clients. You'd be more trusted within your organisation. People would start to ask for your advice and help with larger projects. If you're in sales, people would trust you with bigger accounts and clients would be more convinced by your proposals. If you're on a leadership track, you know that being a great presenter is one of the surest ways to build your reputation and increase your influence.

You know you need to improve, you just don't know *how*.

Don't worry. This book will guide you, and by the end of it you'll have everything you need to deliver excellent, memorable presentations – the kind of presentations that affect audiences and get people talking about you.

Eventually, whatever your industry, sector, or role, by becoming a great presenter you can even achieve that status that makes you almost indispensable – you become known as the 'go-to' person in your field.

How this book will save you time

'If only I had more time…'

Most people who present in business are wasting time. They're wasting their own time because they're reinventing the wheel every time they present. They're wasting their audience's time because they present badly-constructed arguments and incomprehensible slides, all wrapped in a confused mess of business jargon and buzzwords.

Everyone who's ever presented has had the horrible experience of beginning a presentation knowing that they're not really properly prepared for it. Everyone in business has had the experience of someone asking for a 'quick summary' of a proposal or project – perhaps with only a few minutes to prepare. Everyone who has ever watched a presentation has seen presenters who are underprepared. The presenter stumbles and stammers. Their computer fails, or the clicker does. That 'hilarious' YouTube clip they were going to play doesn't work, or the sound is out of sync. Somehow the slides aren't quite in the right order, or the presentation slowly runs out of energy until it fades into a quiet 'So, any questions?'

Many of us think that these problems could be solved if only we had more time. This is not true. We all have the same amount of time in a day. What matters in presenting is not how much time you have to prepare but how efficiently you use that time.

Having a structured process is one of the most efficient ways of saving time when preparing a presentation. You don't need to reinvent the wheel. What it takes to construct and deliver a good presentation is not a mystery.

By the time you've finished this book, worked through the exercises (I suggest using a good old-fashioned notebook for completing the exercises), and tried the techniques, you'll have an almost guaranteed system that will help you construct solid, engaging presentations that speak directly to the needs of the audience and position you as the credible expert. With practice, you'll be able to construct the basics of an excellent presentation in about fifteen minutes – and even get to the stage where you don't need Power-Point!

Why is this book different?

There are many books on presentation skills and public speaking, but this one is different for three main reasons.

Firstly, this book is written from deep experience. I'm not primarily a presentation coach, I'm a public speaker and performer. Presenting is what I do, and have done, for a long time.

Most of my working life is spent presenting to audiences, and before I became a public speaker I worked for nearly twenty years as a magician (yes, that is actually a job and, no, I can't make your beloved disappear).

Whether speaking or performing magic, for all of my adult life I've had to engage audiences, gain rapport, encourage enthusiasm, and get people to pay attention to my message. My ability to do this has been what's paid my mortgage, put food on the table, and given me some great stories.

I've had to learn how to cope with nerves, how to prepare for questions, and how to respond when someone says, 'Oh, could you just talk for fifteen minutes?' with zero preparation time. I've presented in front of a huge variety of audiences – cynical boards, eager young professionals, and loud, confrontational drunks.

I've built my business almost entirely through public presenting – through standing up in front of an audience and saying, 'Here's my idea, and here's why you should act on it.'

I've spoken to audiences of nearly every size – from two people at the end of a telephone line to more than a thousand from a stage. I've had microphones fail, had my timings cut in half a few seconds before I started, and even been introduced as an international tax expert!

I think I've seen, and made, almost every mistake possible in presenting, and I know exactly what it's like to be staring at a blank screen thinking, 'I've got to present this afternoon – *where* do I start?' This book will help you to avoid all of those mistakes and put yourself instantly into the top 10% of presenters.

Secondly, as far as I know, few books on presenting teach you a *system*.

Over the twenty years I've been in this field, I've watched some of the best and worst presenters, I've given thousands of presentations myself, I've worked with hundreds of clients on creating and delivering great presentations, and I've analysed what makes a great presentation work.

Great presentations do not happen by accident; they are always designed. That design can be learnt.

Great presentations fundamentally consist of only two things – a clear, compelling message and an excellent delivery. Both of these things can be broken down into their core parts, and you can learn how to be an expert in each of these core parts.

In this book, you'll learn my MAP process. The MAP process is a complete system that will help you to construct and deliver great presentations easily and quickly.

Thirdly, this book is aimed at a specific audience: busy professionals who want to become great presenters but don't know where to start or how to find the time.

This book addresses the needs of a business audience. You have little time to prepare. There is lots of other stuff on your plate. You're often delivering presentations to people you know well; sometimes they're team members, sometimes other departments, sometimes clients you need to impress. Often, internal politics will have to be factored into the message and delivery.

Your audiences are busy, stressed, and perhaps a little jaded. Sometimes you have to deliver from a 'pitch deck'. You don't just need to be a great presenter, you need to build your reputation and influence.

Why you should present more

Before we get stuck into learning *how* to present better, let's look at *why*.

Imagine Jenny and Jane.

Jenny and Jane are both thirty years old, they work in the same department, and presenting is becoming increasingly important for them. They have to present internally, sometimes with updates, and sometimes to ask for resources, often competing with other departments.

Occasionally, they have to present directly to clients and prospects, especially in pitches where their expertise is a key part of winning the business.

Neither of them enjoys presenting. They both get anxious in the hours before a presentation, and they'd both be delighted if a presentation was cancelled at the last minute.

Jane, however, has decided to do something about it.

Jane had a 'lightbulb' moment while watching a colleague present (by coincidence, it was Jenny!): she noticed that, although everyone gets nervous, Jenny was making everything worse and more difficult than it should be.

It wasn't that Jenny was dreadful, she was just underwhelming. She relied on 'stock' slides to deliver her presentation. She rushed through her delivery, meaning it was difficult to keep up with her. She spoke in a monotone, so it was hard to know which bits were particularly important. She didn't really have a 'message' – her presentation was just a string of facts. She didn't seem particularly interested in taking questions, and no one seemed very interested in asking any.

Jane realised something crucial – this isn't just about the presentation, *it's about Jenny's reputation*. What makes people stand out in business is not (with rare exceptions) their technical skill, it's their ability to get their message across and be heard by others.

Jane made a decision right there. She would learn how to be a better presenter.

She followed the MAP process. She got some coaching to help with her delivery. She asked colleagues for feedback. She deliberately watched good presenters in her field. She watched online videos of great presenters. She improved, and quickly.

Over the next two years, the effect was amazing.

Jenny kept presenting in the same way. She still worked hard, most people liked her, and she did her job. However, she stayed in the same role, and in fact she was passed over for a promotion. A new director was recruited for her department, and while they had a friendly personal relationship Jenny never really got to know the director well. As both were busy people, there didn't seem to be many chances to deepen the relationship.

Jenny slowly became aware that she was being passed a lot of the 'process' jobs, and she was handling logistics for various projects. The number of times she was asked to go on client visits dropped, and when she was invited she was given strict instructions on what to say. On a personal level, she was feeling increasingly like a cog in a machine.

Jane's story is different. Her first couple of presentations were a little wobbly, but she soon got the hang of presenting. She was still nervous, but she knew how to calm her nerves down and focus on her message.

Her presentations became more precise, and better for her audience. Her messages were being listened to more carefully. People started asking more engaged, interesting questions. They began asking her advice on subjects related to her presentations. People looked forward to her presentations because they knew that they were going to get relevant messages that were right for them. She got better with practice.

Jane found that after two or three successful presentations, she was feeling less nervous. Feeling less nervous meant that she could be a bit more daring in her presentations. Being a bit more daring meant that the presentations were more interesting to the audience. More interesting presentations meant that the audience liked Jane more. Because they liked her more, Jane felt less nervous. Because she felt less nervous... (see the beginning of the paragraph).

Jane was asked to go on more and more client visits, and she was handed two large, and sensitive, internal projects. The sales director asked her to take on larger chunks of client presentations, and eventually the company created a new role for her, merging her 'ordinary' work with the ambassadorial role she was now fulfilling.

When the new department director was recruited, Jane was asked to give the first presentation to her – a quick overview of the major projects that were ongoing, as well as an assessment and critique of the strategy that the department had been using over the previous twelve months.

The director loved it and scheduled some follow-up presentations, which quickly turned into peer-level conversations. The director appreciated the fact that Jane could put together credible, incisive messages quickly. Jane, in turn, built on her credibility by delivering great presentations.

At the end of two years, Jane was head-hunted by

another firm. The offer was exciting – a genuinely challenging role in a fast-growing company. Jane told her director about the offer. Two days later, Jane received a counter-offer from her current company: an enhanced role, greater responsibility, and, of course, a salary increase. Jane happily accepted.

In case you haven't guessed, Jane is real. She's a client of mine, and her story is one that I've seen played out in various forms over and over again. Notice that Jane and Jenny both have the same level of education and technical expertise, but Jane is happier, more fulfilled, and more successful.

This is why you should present more. Just being good at something isn't enough anymore – you have to be able to *communicate* what you're good at, and you have to able to communicate in a way that is credible, efficient, and relevant to the audience.

We're all busy, and we're getting busier. In the world of business, rightly or wrongly, we just don't have time to give people the benefit of the doubt anymore. We want answers, solutions, and help right here, right now, and we want to know that we can trust people to do what they say they're going to do when they say they're going to do it.

Being someone who presents well gives you a much greater opportunity to create a positive 'brand' for yourself. By presenting your projects, goals, ideas, successes, and, sometimes, failures, it's easier for you to become a trusted expert.

PERSONAL BRAND

The circus impresario Barnum allegedly said, 'I don't care what they say about me, as long as they get my name right!' Take a lesson from a circus-owner. Given the choice to work with two different people – one who we've seen present well, and one who we know nothing about – we'll nearly always want to work with the person we've seen present.

When you present, you get the chance to do something amazing – you can connect with and influence people in real time. You can convince them of your trustworthiness in minutes. You can take questions, make people think, get buy-in for your ideas, and even make them smile.

You can get people talking to you and about you. You can spread your ideas by word of mouth. You'll find that people will ask for your advice more, listen to you more, and provide you with more opportunities.

This isn't about 'presentation skills'. Nobody is interested in your presentation skills. It's about your ability to connect with other people and get your point across in a way that's meaningful to them. Notice in Jane's story that the director doesn't say, 'Please work more closely with me because of your great presentation skills.'

Presenting is a means to an end – to connecting with an audience and helping them understand something, take action on something, or feel differently about something.

Norman Mailer once said, 'Writers don't get paid to think things up, they get paid to write them down.'

I think a similar thing is true of ideas in business – it's no good having lots of great ideas if you don't know how to communicate them to other people.

Getting out there and presenting your ideas to other people frequently is a genuine win-win. You boost your reputation, your ideas get acted on, and you become 'known' as an expert. But it's not just about you – your team, company, and clients also benefit if your good ideas are acted on. If people see that giving good presentations is a key to career success, then they'll start working harder at being good presenters, and they'll likely look to you for advice and help.

And a world where everyone is a good presenter? Well, that could mean death to 'death by Power-Point'!

Why all presentations are selling something

We are all in the business of sales. Teachers sell students on learning; traditional salespeople sell products. Presenters are often selling ideas, but they're definitely selling. The Busy Person's way to quickly improve any presentation is to remind yourself that whenever you present you are selling something.

How many presentations have you sat through where you had no idea what the point of the presentation was? How many have you sat through where it wasn't clear what the presenter wanted you to do or know? How many have just been a waste of your time?

Far too many for me, and probably for you too. One of the reasons for this is that presenters in business make a common mistake: they assume that presenting is about giving out information. They think that as long as they say some words in the right order and show some slides that they've 'presented'. They haven't. What they've usually done is confuse and bore their audience because they haven't bothered to put any thought into the effect their message has on their audience. They haven't focused on what they're selling.

Of course, not every presentation is selling a product or service. But every presentation is selling something. It might be an idea, or inspiration. If you're getting buy-in for a project, you might be selling the dangers of *not* starting the project. If you're launching a new initiative, you might be selling enthusiasm. If you're presenting to a client, you might be selling trust and credibility.

BE CLEAR ON WHAT YOU'RE SELLING

It's not obvious to many presenters, but most audiences *want* to be sold to. Audiences welcome clear ideas, compelling propositions, and structured arguments. If you're clear on what you're selling, the audience will be too. And, even better, they're likely to buy it.

Think about the next presentation that you have to give in your organisation. What is it that you're selling in this presentation?

Now that you know what you're selling, let's start the process and learn our MAP to great presentations.

The MAP process

Since the days of Aristotle, many people have studied what it takes to construct and deliver speeches and presentations. The art of speaking in public has been studied for thousands of years, and humans already knew almost everything worth knowing about 2,500 years ago.

Aristotle is the granddaddy (or *páppos*, if you want to be Ancient Greek about it) of public speaking. Taking advantage of the sunny Greek days, he wandered around ancient Athens watching great speakers and making a systematic study of the tricks that they used to persuade and engage their listeners. He must have been a busy man, because he managed to note down pretty much every useful trick and tip in the public speaker's notebook – even before notebooks were invented. Some of his terms, like *rhetoric*, have become part of the English language. Others, such as *enthymeme* and *epideictic*, have faded a bit.

Although there are differences of opinion, and some rhetorical techniques have come in and out of fashion (few people present in iambic pentameter anymore, but the elevator pitch is all the rage), there's one consistently recommended technique – structure. Every writer and thinker on speaking in public has emphasised the need to structure a message. The MAP process – **M**essage, **A**udience, **P**resenter – will give you a clear structure that will guide you in the right direction for every presentation.

I've chosen the acronym 'MAP' carefully. Whenever we need direction, a map is a useful guide. When we need direction *and* we have no time to make mistakes, a map becomes essential. This book is your presenting map.

The MAP process is quick and simple, and a guaranteed route to a great presentation. Almost all problems in presenting – knowing how to prepare, dealing with nerves, engaging an audience and getting buy-in for your ideas – can be solved by this structured process. What you're going to learn is a reliable, replicable structure that delivers predictable results.

Chapter One, 'The Message', will explain the importance of engaging the audience emotionally and creating a strong narrative for your presentation. You'll learn why setting a goal is crucial to a successful presentation. We'll cover many of the tricks that performers, script writers, and politicians use to craft great messages. And you'll discover how to make your own message simple, punchy, and memorable.

In Chapter Two, 'The Audience', you'll learn how important it is to see your presentation from the audience's point of view. You'll also learn the essential questions you must ask to make your presentation relevant and engaging for your audience. And you'll see why it's only what the audience takes from your presentation that matters – not what you think you've given them.

In Chapter Three, 'The Presenter', you'll learn the performance tricks that make any presentation a standout. From calming nerves to sounding confident, I'll guide you through the essential skills that great presenters and performers use all the time, and you'll learn a structured 'one-minute warm-up' that will get you psychologically and physically ready for any presentation situation.

As a bonus, I've included two extra chapters – one is dedicated to putting slides together for a presentation, and the other has some advanced tips for big presentations for which you have more time to prepare.

The first time you read this book, read through it in the order suggested, and take your time over the exercises and suggestions. Some of them sound simple, but there's a lot to be learnt from doing them well. A map is a guide, but at some point you have to use it to walk the route. Presenting is the same – it's not enough to read this book. You need to put it into practice.

Occasionally you'll see 'signposts'. These are places on the route where you'll find exercises, reminders, bonus tips, and other ideas to help you keep going in the right direction on your presentation journey.

I recommend the use of stories a lot in this book. I particularly love stories that teach a lesson. As well as the structured steps, you'll find case studies and anecdotes that will inspire you to think differently about presenting. If you take the time to understand the ideas in this book, follow the exercises, and grab opportunities to practise in the real world, you'll be streets ahead of where you are now.

> **SIGNPOST**
>
> Think about the benefit that learning a structure for presentations could give you, and complete this sentence:
>
> 'If I had a reliable, replicable structure for great presentations, I would be able to...'

By the time you finish this book you will:

- Be confident that you can create and deliver an excellent presentation, even with limited preparation time.
- Know how to understand your audience and really 'speak their language'.
- Have a clear understanding of what makes a great message for your audience.
- Know how to make your message stick – for the right reasons.
- No longer be a slave to slides.
- Understand how presenting is one of the most effective and speedy ways to increase your influence and reputation – both internally and with clients.
- Know how to reduce the effects of nerves.
- Understand the importance of good vocal use, and understand how great presenters manage to sound, and act, so charismatic.
- Know how to measure the success of your presentations so that you keep improving.

- Know how to deal with questions.
- Know how to deal with internal rivalries and politics.
- Have a clear checklist so you can't fail.
- Look forward to presenting, because you'll know how many opportunities open up for great presenters.
- Be well on the road to becoming an outstanding communicator.

What's not to like?

CHAPTER ONE

The Message

The importance of the message

Think about the last five business presentations you've seen. What do you remember about them? If they were like most presentations, they'll typically have been unmemorable, irrelevant, too long, full of slides, and delivered in a dreary, uninteresting manner.

Now think of a presentation you've seen that you really liked. What do you remember about it?

When you listen carefully to how people describe good presentations, you'll notice that they're nearly always talking about the *message* and how the message *resonates* with them. In business, after a great keynote speaker, you'll hear people say things like, 'That was so simple, but so true. We really need to take action soon, or we'll be behind the competition,' or, 'I think that clarifies something that we've been avoiding talking about, and we really should face it.'

As an audience, we're always, and only, interested in the parts of any presentation that speak directly to us – to our needs, wants, worries, and hopes. And that means that every great presentation must have a great message. In fact, your message is more important than your 'presentation skills'.

As a speaker, it's always the highest compliment anyone can give me when they say, 'You've really inspired me to *do* something today.' In fact, this is so true that I would think it almost an insult if someone talked to me about my presentation skills rather than my content. Imagine what that would be like: 'Oh hi, I really enjoyed your presentation. I liked your posture and the way you didn't say "Um". I can't remember your message, though. Thanks. Bye.' It would be bizarre, wouldn't it?

Everything in your presentation should centre on your core message and how that message will affect a specific audience. This is so obvious that it shouldn't need stating, but it nearly always comes as a revelation to people giving business presentations because we all get into bad habits so quickly.

So, here's a quick signpost fix. It's both a technique and a way of thinking.

SIGNPOST

When you first know you're going to give a presentation, do not fire up PowerPoint. Instead, write down this phrase:

'Don't think of what I want to say, think of what the audience *needs to hear.*'

Keep this phrase in front of you as you start working on your message. In our MAP analogy, this phrase is your compass and will keep you on the right track.

Next, you need to know what the *core* of your message is. Where's the presentation headed, and what's the end goal? Luckily, a Busy Person can find this out by asking a single question.

How to find your message with a single question

The Busy Person's way of getting to the core of your presentation quickly starts with this question:

'What do I want my audience to do (and to know and to feel) as a result of my presentation?'

I ask this question every time I begin to work on a presentation, and I use it with all of my clients. I have never yet come across a presentation that can't be improved by using this question to create a goal.

It's important not to skip over this step. In fact, if you really answer this question well, then you'd almost be in a position to create an off-the-cuff presentation at very short notice. (Don't worry, I'm not asking you to do that – yet!)

In the question, I've written the three words *do, know,* and *feel* in that order for a reason. It's crucial that you address the word *do* – the other two are useful, but *do* is essential. One of the things I've noticed in my coaching work with clients is that many people can quickly address the *know* question, but they still haven't got a real goal yet.

Here's an example:

I was working with a partner in a digital marketing agency; I'll call him John. (That's not his real name. His real name is Peter.) The agency was due to present a proposal to a prospective client. This was an important presentation for them, with a lot of work riding on the outcome. In John's own words: 'I'm a partner, and I'm being wheeled out to make sure the client knows we're serious.'

When we started working together, I asked John to show me the ten minutes that he'd planned. As is so often the case, it was just a lot of 'stuff' about him and his company. It was full of irrelevant historical details, jargon about the company, and nothing that was of benefit to the audience.

His opening went something like this:

'Hi everyone, my name's John, and I'm a partner at ABC Ltd. We specialise in digital marketing campaigns. What we believe in is passion for what we do and we're different to other agencies because of our attention to detail, and our commitment to getting a good result for our clients. Over the last ten years, we've worked with lots of clients, in various sectors and we...'

I won't put you through the rest, but it was ten minutes more of that. It sounded good – to him! But if you were the audience for this presentation, you'd be zoning out quickly as the wave of forgettable corporate jargon washed gently over your head.

Many – far too many – presentations begin like this. A pile of information, verbal sludge, none of it targeted very well towards the audience. Worse, he was leaving his colleagues with an uphill task. His colleagues were going to have to work hard to get the audience's attention back.

John and I talked briefly about his audience. It was clear that he had a reasonably good sense of who the audience was, so that wasn't the problem. Then I asked John what his goal was. He told me, 'Well, I want them to *know* about our company and that we're the right fit for them.' He had a rough goal in mind, but it wasn't clear, and this created an unclear presentation.

Many people have 'give information' as a rough goal for their presentations:

- I need to tell my team about the strategy.
- I need everyone to understand the new compliance requirements.
- I need to bring everyone up to speed on where the project is at.

But 'giving information' is not good enough. Listing information is almost always the *worst* way to present.

Also, how can you measure this goal? How can you be certain that your team have now learnt the strategy and have bought into it? How can you be certain that everyone 'understands' the new compliance requirements? How can you be sure that everyone is 'up to speed' on where the project is at?

I hope you can see that these are unmeasurable goals. It's hard to know whether you've achieved them fully, or at all.

Let's look at what happens when you focus on *do* as a goal:

I asked John: 'Ok, what do you want the audience to *do* as a result of this presentation?'

JOHN: 'Well, I want them to know that we're the right fit.'

ME: 'Two things – you've re-told me your *know* goal. That's not a measurable goal. Secondly, do you really think you can achieve that goal in ten minutes? If so, why are the rest of your team presenting for another forty minutes?'

JOHN: 'Oh, I see. Well, I suppose I want the audience to listen carefully to what's coming next.'

ME: '*That's* closer to becoming a goal. What else? How do you want the audience to *feel*?'

JOHN: 'Well, I want them to feel excited and intrigued by what they're about to hear.'

ME: 'Ok, so if you combine those two, you've now got a decent goal for your part of the presentation.'

JOHN: 'I want the audience to feel excited and intrigued, so that they'll be ready to listen carefully to my colleagues.'

Go back and re-read John's original presentation opening with this new goal in mind, and see how what he'd prepared falls short in almost every way.

When John focused on this new goal, his presentation began like this:

> 'Hello everyone. My name's John and, as I'm a partner at ABC, I'm sure you're all expecting me to talk about how marvellous we are, and so on, but actually I'm going to do the opposite. I'm going to talk about you – particularly, three problems that we think you're facing.
>
> 'Firstly, what we're seeing in the marketplace with companies like yours is that there's often a problem with internal worries about digital marketing: What if we get it wrong? Is it worth it? My colleague, Emma, is going to show you our research on why this occurs and what you can do about it.
>
> 'Secondly, we know from some benchmarking data we've collated that in terms of usability, ease, and conversion rates, your website currently ranks around twenty-seventh out of one hundred of your competitors. That's not a disaster, but I'm sure you'd like to improve it! Dave is going to take you through a quick case study of another of our clients who went from fifty-second to third place in fourteen months. He'll also show you the process we use to get these repeatable results.

'Finally, we know how difficult it is to get internal buy-in to many digital marketing projects. We've been helping clients launch, and succeed with, projects for nearly twenty years, and Andy here is going to give you some important information that you can use to get buy-in internally – whether you work with us or not.

'I'll be here to take questions at the end. We don't want this presentation to be too formal; we hope that, as well as hearing our pitch, you'll learn something useful to take away and use internally straight away. Does that sound good to everyone? Ok, Emma – over to you...'

This time, everything is aimed towards achieving his main goal: 'To make the audience feel excited and intrigued and to make them listen carefully to my colleagues.'

The presentation this time felt snappy and focused. Really try and think about this from the audience's point of view – they've come in expecting to hear a sales pitch. They've probably heard two sales pitches already from competing firms, and they've likely got a few more lined up. But this isn't a sales pitch – it's something that's useful to them.

John knew, from the audience analysis that he'd done, that the prospective client was facing significant internal problems in terms of convincing the leadership team to buy into the idea of focusing on digital marketing.

He also knew that there were likely to be significant 'politics' going on in the room. Three of the five attendees were already committed to *some* change, and the only decision they needed to make was which vendor to use. Two of the attendees, however, were senior members of the firm who had not been involved in any of the preparatory work on the pitch. It was safe to assume that they weren't just judging my client – they were also judging their colleagues, and perhaps the whole idea of this expensive project in the first place.

Look over the new presentation opening again, and see how well it not only achieves the goal of getting the audience excited and intrigued about what's coming next but also solves some of the audience's problems – before the presentation has even begun.

John told me that the effect on the audience of this new style was terrific. In fact, when John asked, 'Does that sound good to everyone?' the most senior person in the room said, 'Definitely!' It was clear from his tone that this was a refreshing start rather than a dreary sales pitch.

More importantly, John said that his status as a partner increased because he'd stopped 'selling' and was simply helping the prospective client.

Use this question to set a goal for your presentation every time – 'What do I want my audience to *do* (and *know*, and *feel*) as a result of this presentation?'

The answer to this question not only gives you your goal for your presentation – it will also help you answer many of the questions that tend to come up when preparing a presentation, such as: 'Do I need slides?' Well, what do you want the audience to *do*? Until you've answered that question, you don't know if you need slides or not.

Having a clear goal lets you assess the success of your presentation *during* and *after* the presentation. If you're clear about what you want your audience to *do* as a result of your presentation, then you'll know when they're not doing it, and you can deal with that during the presentation itself.

In the example above, John's goal was to get the audience interested enough that they'd be listening carefully to what was coming next. It was his job to get them into that state before handing over to his colleague.

He achieved that goal, and it was easy for him to see that he'd achieved it just by looking around the room. However, if he'd failed to achieve it, that would also have been obvious. People would have been distracted or looked uninterested, maybe doodling or responding to emails. In that case, John could still have dealt with it to some extent. If you don't know what your goal is in the first place, though, you can't tell that you're not achieving it.

John's original goal was 'to tell them enough so they know we're a good fit'. Well, he can't know if he is, or isn't, achieving that goal during the presentation, so he can't know whether or not he should change his approach or add or subtract any information.

When clients tell me vague goals, I always ask, 'How will you know whether you've achieved that goal?'

It's at this point that people start to hesitate, pause, and stammer, 'Well, erm, I think that as long as I cover the essentials, they'll have everything they need.'

I then reply: 'Ok, but that doesn't answer the

question. How will you *know* that you've "covered the essentials" – from the audience's point of view?'

It soon becomes obvious that there's no way to know. And, as any shiny-suited consultant will tell you, if you can't measure a goal it's hard to achieve it.

There is a difference, though, if I insist on *do* as the main word in the goal – 'What do you want your audience to *do*?' Sales people, for example, might answer: 'As a result of my presentation, I want my audience to know enough about my company, and our service, *to agree to another meeting with senior execs,*' Or, if you're giving an internal update, the goal might be: 'I want the audience to know enough that they can trust my team to deliver and *will recommend starting the project.*'

The change is really simple, but knowing your real end goal can transform everything in your presentation and help you to avoid common mistakes.

Often in presentations, people talk too much about themselves and their own offering. If you think clearly about the first goal above, however, it becomes obvious that everything in your presentation should help your audience relay your message internally. This means you've got to simplify your message and really consider the following: 'Which bits of my presentation are memorable and interesting enough to be sent "up the chain"?'

With the sales goal above, it becomes clear: the absent audience of senior execs are the focus of this presentation, and the current audience are just a means to an end! Sorry if that sounds harsh, but don't worry – by working on your presentation in this way, you'll give the current audience a better, more precise and more interesting presentation anyway, so everyone's better off.

Lastly, if you had this sales goal it would be clear that you have to excite and interest the current audience, but you have to leave enough unsaid to get the second meeting. The current presentation has to be focused on 'selling the future', but you need to leave the question of 'How do we achieve that?' for a future meeting.

Leaving information out is not a natural thing to do. In fact, most people's instinct when presenting is to fill the presentation with too much information. When you're clear on your goal, though, it becomes obvious what information should be left out, and what should be included.

One of my clients had exactly this goal of securing a second meeting. They seeded their presentation with statements such as:

> 'So, that's the main outcome that would be achieved, and we've given you an approximate guide as to how we'd do it. Obviously, there'd be a lot more detail to go into, which is probably best left until we've all confirmed that we want to do this.'

and:

> 'Clearly, if this meeting goes well, you'll be at a stage when you're going to have to get buy-in internally, and we've got a presentation that is aimed at that stage, which we're happy to talk you through at the end of this meeting.'

This wording wouldn't be appropriate for all presentations, and it will depend on your personal style, but the point remains – until you're clear on your goal, you can't make *any* decisions with confidence. At best you'll be bluffing, and at worst you'll deliver a presentation that wastes everyone's time and lowers your long-term credibility.

There's one final benefit to this goal-oriented approach. Often, once you've got your goal, you can *tell* your audience what your goal is word for word.

Put yourself in the audience's shoes. When someone tells you their goal, it makes it much easier for you to understand how the whole presentation relates to you and your world.

For example:

> 'As a result of this presentation, I'd love you to be confident that you've got all the information you need from us to make a decision about whether to take this forward or not.'

> 'As a result of this presentation, I want all of you to have a clear view of where management want to take the company over the next eighteen months. I want all of you to see where your ideas are already being implemented and how to make your voice heard as we roll out the new strategy.'

> 'By the end of this presentation, you'll understand why our research matters, and, more importantly, you'll know how to use it effectively when contacting your clients.'

Creating a clear, action-based goal is extremely useful for busy people because it saves you time by getting right to what matters quickly – and you can start right now.

SIGNPOST

For the next presentation you have coming up, write down and complete the sentence:

What I want my audience to *do* as a result of my presentation is...

You'll be amazed at how quickly and easily this clarifies your thinking and helps you focus on what's important.

SIGNPOST

For any presentation, before you do anything else, clarify your message. You should be able to complete the following sentences for each presentation:

'In this presentation, I'm selling...'

'As a result of this presentation, I want my audience to be able to...'

'I'll know I've achieved my goal because the audience will...'

Make sure your presentation goal is:

· Clear and written down.

- Focused on action.

- Simple and easy to communicate.

- Measurable (I'll know when I've got it).

- Appropriate and relevant for the specific audience.

- Achievable in the time allowed for the presentation.

How to structure your message and make it flow

Clarifying your core message has taken you a long way on your journey to a successful presentation. However, we've all seen presentations where the core message is pretty good but where, as the audience, we've still had to make an effort to find what the message is because the presenter hasn't structured it clearly enough for us.

Let's look at another example presenter, Sally, who asked me to work with her on a new client presentation she had to deliver. Sally was a naturally good presenter in most respects. She spoke well and had a natural ability to get on with her audience. She was a 'people person'.

But when she presented to me it was clear that her argument was confused, and the value of her proposal was diluted by badly-arranged arguments, too much information, and a weak ending. The service her company provided was excellent, and the core offering (once we could understand it clearly) was great. But the message was buried in a muddle.

Our old culprit PowerPoint is largely to blame. Sally had started work on her presentation by grabbing some slides from previous presentations and moving them around into something she thought looked good, filling in a few gaps as she went.

Many people present like Sally did. There's probably a decent message hidden somewhere, but it's buried under 'verbal rubble'. This matters, because audiences won't make any effort for you. If they have to do any mental work, they'll just switch off, or they'll assume that your message isn't credible.

The following is a format for structuring a presentation that I find useful, as do many of my clients. Its power lies in its simplicity. You can take this format with you anywhere and use it for any presentation. Regardless of whether you have to do a quick two-minute speech or a two-hour-long sales presentation, this structure will always help you.

1. Start with a clean sheet of paper. I have no idea why, but a crisp, clean sheet of paper seems to do wonders for boosting creativity and breaking bad habits when working on a presentation. If your presentation is short and simple, then a notepad will do. If you've got lots of ideas, and a long presentation, then a sheet of flip-chart paper is ideal.

2. At the top of the paper, draw a box.

3. In the box, write your main goal – you need to have this visible at all times.

4. Then, draw a straight line down from the bottom of your box, make a second box (linked to the first box by the line) and write 'Intro/Hook' in it.

5. From the second box, draw three lines – one to the left, one straight down, and one to the right, and create one additional box at the other end of each of those lines. Name these three new boxes 'Point 1 – Story/Anecdote', 'Point 2 – Data/rationale', and 'Point 3 – Audience Relevance', respectively.

6. Under the three boxes, create a box marked 'Summary?'

7. Under the summary box draw another box that contains only a question mark.

8. Then, draw a final box near the bottom of the page, and call it 'Punchline'.

And that's it – the structure for a great presentation. You're thinking, 'It can't be that simple!' – but it really can.

In this structure, you have a skeleton on which you can hang the main arguments. You may want to extend the structure and make it a bit longer, but you'll never want it to be shorter.

Why does it work so well? This is a structure that has been around for as long as humans have been trying to persuade each other. Some of the ideas here date back to Aristotle.

We've already covered your main goal, but you need to have it visible when working on your presentation so that you stay focused on where you're headed and why.

A good presentation needs a hook, because you only have a short amount of time to gain your audience's attention and interest, and so you need to be clear that your introduction is not just information but is designed to 'hook' your audience quickly and effectively. We'll cover the hook in more detail in the next section.

The next three boxes will contain your three main points. You might, eventually, want to add another point or two, but for now, stick to the discipline of three.

Sometimes you'll need a summary, and at other times you may not – that's why the summary box has a question mark after it. The question mark box is also the right place to take questions from the audience.

Lastly, you need a 'punchline'. We'll look at this in more depth in a later section, but the main point is that you have to finish well. Many people assume that the end of the presentation is an excuse to sum up what's happened and then ask for questions. See the section of this chapter entitled 'Always have a punchline' to find out why that's not always the best approach.

First, though, let's look at the 'hook'...

Hook the audience

How much easier would your professional life be if you were an outstanding presenter? If everyone you worked with treated you as a credible expert and listened carefully to everything you had to say? If people really *got* what your projects were about? Well, you can be!

The section-opening paragraph above is a 'hook'. Using a hook will turn you instantly into a world-class presenter.

How many times have you heard presentations that begin:

> 'Good morning everyone, thanks for coming today. Well, basically I'm going to tell you about our survey we've conducted, and then I'll show some graphs with all the data, and then hopefully we can show you what our plans are for the next quarter.'

or:

> 'Hi everyone, so we're here to tell you about our service today. We're a full-service marketing agency, and we were founded in 1987 by John Smith. Today, we've got over thirty clients, and we work all over Europe. We've won prizes...'

We've all experienced presentation openings like these. They're not illegal, and no one's going to die because of them, but they're ineffective.

Worse than ineffective, they're also wasteful – they waste the golden opportunity you're given at the beginning of your presentation. When you start a presentation, you've got everything going for you – the audience are hopeful, awake, and expectant. They're inclined to give you a fair hearing.

So many presenters waste this opportunity by filling the start of their presentations with boring 'stuff' that is irrelevant and uninteresting. They turn audiences off for a simple reason: audiences do not want to make any mental effort. If, at the start of your presentation, they feel like they're going to have to work to understand your message, you will quickly lose their attention.

You are a step ahead, though, because you've done your prep work and clarified your goal. Now, you're going to apply that to the first moments of your presentation.

You need a hook for several reasons:

- The audience want to feel like it's going to be easy and interesting to listen to your presentation.

- The audience members have one question on their minds – 'What's in this for me?'

- Audiences do not expect a hook, so your presentation becomes instantly better than most if you have one.

- A good hook can tie a whole presentation together because it can open ideas in an audience's mind that you can refer to later.

I normally recommend spending up to 5% of your total presentation time on the introduction, but aim to have something that hooks your audience as soon as you can, certainly within the first minute or so.

In your structure skeleton document, in the box marked 'Intro/Hook' write down the main point you want your audience to take away from your presentation. (You know what this is because of your work on the goal.)

Ask yourself, 'If I were the audience, how would I react to this point?' If the answer is 'Really well', then you've already got your hook. For example:

'In this presentation I'm going to cover three main points, but I know from our previous conversations that you're most concerned about whether we can get this project finished by August. By the end of this presentation, you'll have the answer to that question – and it might surprise you.'

This is a great hook. The audience has been told that their needs are understood, and they're going to be addressed. There's no fluff or filler here. Emotionally, you feel that 'this is going to be a good presentation, and a good use of my time'.

Sometimes, though, it won't be as simple as telling your audience your main point. Your aim might be more to inspire, educate, or influence your audience. In these cases, the following types of hook can work wonderfully.

An intriguing, provocative, or rhetorical question

Audiences love questions, don't they? Especially questions that confirm what they already know in an interesting way or help them see what they already know in a new way.

In fact, questions are such a sure-fire method for hooking an audience's attention that I'm surprised more people don't use them more often, aren't you?

I give a presentation on becoming more persuasive in business, and near the beginning of the session I ask the audience: 'Imagine that you could, suddenly, become really persuasive. What difference would that make? How would your life be different?'

I then give the audience about thirty seconds to turn that over in their minds. When I ask for feedback, people often say that this moment was very powerful and important for them. I refer back to this moment later in the presentation, when I ask the audience:

'Do you remember when I asked you to consider what your own lives would be like if you could be super-persuasive? In that moment, you conjure up your own vision of what that means to you, which is far more persuasive than anything I could say to you.'

I've used a question as my hook to gain everyone's interest at the start, and then I've 'closed' that hook later in the presentation. It's very satisfying for the audience, and it helps them to remember my point much better.

Can rhetorical questions work well? I'm glad you asked. Yes, they can. They can provoke the audience to think deeply about a subject or focus their minds on what's important. For example: 'It's easy to talk about success in this industry, but hard to achieve it. In what ways are we holding ourselves back?'

Rhetorical questions can be very effective at engaging emotion. For example, instead of saying, 'We all know that sales can be an uphill struggle', a presenter might ask, 'When was the last time anyone here thought, "This sales business is too easy, I need a bigger challenge"?'

Questions aren't a guarantee of success, and if they're not used well they can work against you. Guard against the following:

A question that is too provocative. For example, 'Why are you all here instead of getting on with some real work?' or, 'Come on, you know we're going to do a sales presentation, but you've got to admit, we're pretty cool already, aren't we?' I'm not making that last one up – I once heard someone say almost exactly that at the beginning of a sales pitch. They didn't get the work.

A question that seems to be rhetorical but is not clear, so the audience are unsure of whether or not they should respond. I avoid this by telling people how they should respond: 'I'm going to ask you a question. I don't need the answer out loud, this is just for you to think about...' When you instruct the audience clearly, they benefit because they don't need to think about how to respond, but you also benefit because the audience will take you more seriously as a presenter. It's one of the many signs of a great presenter that they are in control of what happens.

A question that is too vague, or patronising: 'How many of you agree that we should be doing better?' This kind of question will almost certainly set the audience against you from the start since you'll appear to be either treating them as stupid or else they'll think, 'Oh God, is the whole presentation going to be like this?' Even worse, they may start to find problems with your argument straight away.

Questions that go on so long that the audience has lost the point: For example, 'There's something I'd like you to consider, and this was sparked by a comment my father made many years ago, while we were sitting by a lake on holiday...' [Ten minutes later.] 'So, do you agree with my father?' I've exaggerated, but a lot of presenters make this mistake. Even worse, they don't realise they've made a mistake because audiences *will* respond to a question like this. They *will* put their hands up. The presenter thinks, 'Great, they're really engaged.' The audience is thinking, 'At least if we put our hands up, we might be able to get this over with quickly.'

Simple, interesting questions work well as hooks, so put one in your next presentation. What's stopping you?

A quotation or inspirational comment

Quotations are an excellent way of grabbing an audience's attention. I give a presentation on creating an impact within organisations by building a strong personal brand. I nearly always start the presentation like this:

Jeff Bezos, the founder of Amazon, has a great phrase about personal branding. He says, 'Your personal brand is what people say about you when you're not in the room.' Just reflect for a moment. What are people saying about you when you're not in the room?

This works well as a hook (and notice that I've combined it with a question). The reason it works so well is that the quotation is credible, and when you use credible quotations you boost your own credibility as a speaker.

The quotation also speaks directly to the audience's world. This hook affects people. As soon as I present the quotation, people start thinking, 'Wow, that's true. I wonder what people are saying about *me*!'

This is a true hook, in that the audience are now genuinely 'hooked' on hearing what's coming next. They feel, very quickly, that a problem has been presented, and they are interested to hear the solution. Also, the benefits of getting this solution are clear to them.

An ideal quotation will have some of the following characteristics:

It will be from a famous or credible source. If the source is good, the audience will trust it, and you, more.

It won't be *too* famous or clichéd. Audiences want to feel that they're learning something new, rather than being treated like schoolchildren.

It will be pithy. It will sum up something the audience already knows, but in a new way that's easy to understand quickly. If a quotation needs explaining, it's not a good one to use for a hook.

It will be humorous or thought provoking. A quotation should have that magic quality of making people laugh or think, but not in an obvious way.

It will have a meaning that can be 'unpacked'. This is important, as ideally you'll want to refer to this quotation a couple of times throughout your presentation and again at the end (see the 'Always have a punchline' section of this chapter). Each time that you refer back to the quotation, the meaning should be slightly amplified. For example, when I use the Jeff Bezos quotation above, I refer to it again in relation to people's lives professionally, then personally, and then later I ask them to reflect on what they say about other people when they're 'not in the room'. So, by the end of the presentation, there are at least three layers to this quotation.

It will be easy to remember. This is crucial. Everything in your presentation should be as easy to remember as possible since this increases the chance of your message being retained and passed on. When you listen to audiences talking about a presentation they've liked, you'll often hear them talk about, and repeat, the quotation used.

Try a quotation as your hook. As Borges wrote: 'Life itself is a quotation'.

But there are also a number of quotation mistakes to avoid:

A quotation designed to make you look cleverer than the audience. A quotation that is clumsy, difficult to understand, or just helps the presenter to show off will turn an audience off and reduce your credibility.

Reading the quotation from a slide. By all means add the quotation to your hand-out, or click on a slide that includes the quotation *after* you've given it, but never read it from a slide to the audience. This is partly for performance reasons, but also because you're trying, at the 'hook' stage, to make an emotional connection with your audience and boost your credibility. If you say the quotation without a slide, you'll appear credible, knowledgeable, and competent. If you have to look at your slide to read a simple quotation, you'll reduce your credibility.

Getting the quotation wrong. Ok, this is an obvious one, but you *have* to learn the quotation. I rarely advocate learning a script in presenting, but this is an exception. You have to know the quotation word for word.

Failing to do your research. There's no excuse, now that we're all acquainted with Mr Google, not to know the source of your quotation. It's always a good idea to check the source on a couple of reputable quotation sites to make sure that you're attributing properly. Also, never let yourself say, 'I think it was Churchill who said…' *You* are the presenter, it's *your* responsibility to know the source of your quotations. If you really can't find out, it's better to say, 'A phrase often attributed to Churchill is…'

Giving a 'loaded' quotation. This is particularly unwise when you're dealing with large groups. Avoid anything (no matter how strongly you personally feel) that displays political, religious, or other views that are easy to disagree with or are contentious.

Giving a 'jokey' quotation. There is a world of difference between 'humour' and 'jokes'. I'll explore this in the section titled 'You're joking' in Chapter Three, but jokes are always risky. You have to have excellent timing and a good sense of the audience to make jokes work. Also, avoid any 'jokey' quotations that could be perceived as racist, sexist, or homophobic. I prefer humorous quotations to jokes. These are the quotations that put a gentle smile on people's faces, rather than seeking full-out laughs.

An unusual fact

Did you know that no one was ever burned as a witch in England?

Interesting, isn't it? I bet you'd like to check up on that right away.[1]

Unusual facts or statements can work well as an opening hook – especially ones that have at least one of the following characteristics:

- It is easy to understand.

- It makes the audience see something they knew before, but in a surprising way.

- It is easy to relate back to throughout the presentation.

- It opens a 'mystery' in the audience's mind, making them think, 'That's interesting, where is this going?'

- It contains a counter-intuitive statistic or fact.

- It contains humour (eg 'Statistically, at least 30% of you are already wondering when the coffee is coming.')

- It gets the audience involved – sometimes something

---

1. I've checked for you. Witches were drowned, hanged, tortured, and mistreated in horrible ways but never burned in England. Scotland is another matter.

as simple as asking the audience to move or handing out a prop can act as enough of a surprise to hook the audience.

If someone was presenting about changes in mobile technology, a great hook might be: 'In the Western world, 90% of adults look at their mobile phones at least once every eleven minutes. That means almost all of you will be tempted to look at your phones at least twice while I'm presenting.'

This works well, because it's a fact that everyone can relate to, it relates to the rest of the presentation, it reminds the audience that their customers are identical to them, and – with the right amount of charm – the last sentence is also nicely humorous.

Like everything in presenting, though, if unusual facts are used as a gimmick they lose their effectiveness.

Avoid the following types of facts:

- A fact that is too strange, or irrelevant (for example, 'Did you know that Marconi invented the radio a year earlier than everyone thinks?')

- A fact that is too difficult for an audience to grasp quickly. I once heard someone start a presentation with an explanation of the counter-intuitive nature of exponentiality – I'm not joking. It was unusual, but it didn't do the presenter any favours.

- A fact that is only there for its shock value and doesn't add anything to, or relate to, the rest of your presentation.

- As with quotations, avoid anything with political

or religious views, or anything that could be seen to be racist, sexist, or homophobic.

A funny thing happened on the way here...

Telling a quick anecdote can be a great way of hooking the audience. This technique is used a lot by comedians.

I was working a couple of years ago with someone who pitches to publishers. She had a difficult concept to pitch to them – her business model was potentially competitive to the publishers she was pitching to, even though she was pitching for them to partner with her.

Her business was based on the idea that publishing is on the verge of massive digital change, and her product was an answer to this change. But the change hadn't hit publishing in a big way when she started pitching her solution.

Her early ideas had been to 'sell the benefits' of her solution, but this fell on deaf ears. She tried the 'scare them so they'll buy' model of persuasion, but this had the effect of making the publishers feel like she was trying to teach Grandma to suck eggs.

Together, we came up with the following: she told them a brief anecdote about a business model that once dominated the Western world. That industry was similar to publishing. Everyone bought from it, and the high street was full of shops based on it. People earned billions from it. The model hadn't substantially changed for decades. Then, almost overnight, digital hit this business. Within two years, there were no shops selling this product on the high street, and physical sales of the product were almost non-existent.

As you've probably guessed, this industry is the music industry. Specifically, sales of CDs and records.

My client finished the anecdote by saying:

> 'The record industry didn't see it coming. It's taken them ten years to understand the problem and start to deal with it. In retrospect, it should have been obvious that it was coming. Anyone who'd been able to see the problem and been prepared would now be ten years ahead of the rest.
>
> 'We believe that publishing is in almost exactly the same situation now that the record industry was in a decade ago, and we think the same, or similar, problems are going to hit your industry. We've built this solution to be ahead of the problem and make sure that you're keeping your readers, no matter where they choose to view content.'

If you're a publisher, it's a great hook, because it's clear and easy to relate to, but the presenter hasn't presumed to know more about your industry than you do.

It's important at the 'hook' stage that the anecdote is brief, and the point is clear. There'll be plenty of time to tell longer stories later.

A picture paints...

A good presentation is like a strong espresso. It wakes me up!

That sentence would work as a hook, because it paints a quick picture that the audience can relate to.

Finding a quick metaphor, analogy, or image can grab the audience's attention and ensure that they're easily able to follow the thread of your argument. If you can describe an ideal situation, or make the problem they're facing visual and impactful, you'll often have a winning hook.

Ideally, the illustration will have the following qualities:

- It will be visual and easy to grasp.
- It will be brief.
- It will be memorable.
- It will be easy for people to repeat to others who aren't watching the presentation.

If you're stuck for an idea, try completing the following sentences:

- 'Imagine if...'
- 'Picture this...'
- 'What would it be like if...?'
- 'Wouldn't it be great if...?'

The power of a visual hook is that you can keep referring back to it throughout your presentation, which reinforces the point and makes it easier to remember you and your argument.

For example, if I'd used the 'espresso' example at the beginning of my presentation, I might refer back to it occasionally saying things like, 'If a presentation is the espresso, then slides are like sugar – not always essential, but sometimes needed.'

Slides and props

Using slides or props as a hook is not for the faint-hearted, but it can be effective.

A 'prop' is anything physical that you might display, or use, during your presentation. A prop in this case could be a new piece of technology, a comedy photograph, or a toy used to make a point.

Sometimes, though, a slide can be the best way to 'hook' your audience. For example, in one particular presentation I give the theme is quite mysterious. All people know is that they're going to learn some 'mind skills' from a magician. So, my first hook for this presentation is a slide. When people enter the room, the screen says: 'On your chair is an envelope with a question mark on it. PLEASE DON'T OPEN THE ENVELOPE.'

I won't ruin the surprise of what's in the envelope (you'll have to come and see the session yourself!) but you can imagine the effect it has on the audience – they're instantly curious.

This approach works well for large audiences, or for those who don't know each other well yet. One of my clients needed to ask some questions during her presentation, but she knew that people tended to be a little shy about responding quickly to the questions. So she put up a slide for people to read as they came in. It read, 'We'll start the presentation with a few questions today. The most important one is: "What are the three biggest barriers to successfully onboarding graduates in our business?" Please take a moment to discuss this with someone near you.'

This slide is a great hook because it focuses people's minds on the subject of the presentation, but also helps to avoid those uncomfortable 'I've got to get to know you' moments for the audience. The start of the presentation was a high-energy guided discussion, which lead neatly into what my client wanted to talk about.

One last example: sometimes you can use a single image to make a strong point as your hook. I've seen people use a polar bear stranded on an ice island to make a point about global warming, and an insurance company used a picture of a polluted river near a school to hammer home the need to talk about environmental insurance.

'Show, don't tell' is an old rule of dramatic writing, and it can serve you well in business presenting.

SIGNPOST

Take a moment to write down a hook for your next presentation. Use the following checklist to strength-test the hook, and make sure that your hook ticks at least three items on the list.

Does your hook:

- Wake your audience up (grab their attention)?
- Surprise them?

- Tell them something they already know, but in a new or surprising way?

- Make them laugh or smile?

- Give them information that will make them look good in front of other people?

- Directly answer the question 'What's in it for me?'

- Seem prepared, confident, and fluid?

In general, avoid a hook that:

1. Looks unprepared or rushed.

2. Is all about the presenter, or the presenter's interests.

3. Fails to 'make a connection' with the audience.

4. Makes the audience think, 'This is going to be long, dull, and hard work.'

5. Makes the audience think, 'This is not a good use of my time.'

The Rule of Three

Congratulations – you know what your main message is and you have a hook, so you've already completed more than half the work (this is *The Busy Person's Guide*, remember).

The next step on our journey is to 'shape' the message so that the audience can understand it quickly and easily. The quickest, simplest, and most reliable way to do this is to break the message into three parts. There are some very good reasons for doing this.

THE RULE OF THREE IS EVERYWHERE

Remember when you were last in a restaurant with seemingly endless choices on the menu. How often did you skip from one part of the menu to another? How often did you read the same food item, because you kept looking across at different options, trying to compare them and see how they'd stack up against each other? What about large supermarkets, or film listings on Netflix? Have you ever heard someone say, 'Oh, it's too complicated, I can't decide'? It happens all the time.

Eventually you do decide because you're sitting in a restaurant, you have a shopping list, or you're getting ready to chill, but for many people that decision is more stressful than it needs to be and takes longer than it should.

Conversely, think of what it's like to be only offered one option. I'm a vegetarian, so I'd never even bother looking for something to eat in a steakhouse. I'm sure they'd have one option for me, but that's not enough. I want to feel like I have a choice.

It's not limited to restaurants, supermarkets, or Netflix, of course. We see the Rule of Three all the time in real life. Too much choice is confusing, whereas only having a 'yes/no' option can make us say no in order to feel safe.

There are some lessons here for business presenting, and these lessons apply to your main argument as well as any options you leave people with:

1. Too much choice makes our brains work hard, and people will find it harder to believe your message.

2. Not enough choice can make people stop listening or make them choose the 'no' option.

3. A small number of clear points or a small number of clear options will be memorable, easy to understand, and easy to engage with (that's a list of three!).

If you only give one argument, you could sound like you lack credibility. But if you give a long list of details and arguments, you'll sound confused, and it will be hard for the audience to pick their way through your message and make sense of it for themselves. Audiences do not like making an effort to understand a message. If they have to make the effort it will often undermine your credibility and make it harder for them to engage with your message.

WHY THREE, RATHER THAN FOUR OR FIVE?

There just seems to be something about ideas in threes that our brains 'like'. Occasionally, you might need to have a fourth or even a fifth point, but I encourage you to use three whenever possible.

Threes are memorable – many great speeches build their ideas in groups of threes, children's fairy tales are full of threes (three bears, three elves, three wishes), and so on. In politics, you'll hear the phrase, 'Life, liberty, and the pursuit of happiness'. In France: '*Liberté, égalité, fraternité*'. Think of the most classic beginning to a joke: 'An Englishman, a Scotsman, and an Irishman walk into a bar...'

You'll see it all the time in advertising copy: 'Our online storage keeps your files safe, synced, and easy to share'.

Threes are everywhere. So, the lesson in presenting is not to fight it but to use it to your advantage. This is why I've suggested that you break your main message down into three points, and we'll cover how to do that in the next section.

All great presenters and speech writers use threes a lot. They use threes because they're compelling, creative, and credible. (Sorry, I can't help myself!)

Some of you reading this will be thinking, 'But I have a *lot* more than three points to cover in my presentation.' And you're right. Sometimes you'll have messages that have huge amounts of information in them. You might be describing a complex process, or workflow, or using lots of case studies. Perhaps there's a lot of technical data.

The point about threes still stands. In fact, it's even more advisable in complex presentations to try to break things down into threes. Even intelligent, knowledgeable audiences like to have information presented in a way that is as clear and simple as it can be.

For example, if you're going to present your audience with a complex process, you'll almost certainly lose your audience if you begin:

'So, the process begins at step one, and then we move on to step two, after that step three, and once we've done that, it's step four, then step five...'

If you've got forty-three steps, you will have lost your audience to daydreams long before you've reached the end.

Thinking in terms of threes, though, you could break it down into:

'I'm going to take you through our process, it's a fairly lengthy one, but there are three main elements to it:

'First, the work to make new customers aware of you. Second, the project work that you deliver. Third, the follow-up once the project is finished, to maintain loyalty.

'So, step one in bringing your market to you is…'

This is much clearer for your audience. It allows them to concentrate more, because they're given a sense of where the journey of this process is taking them.

In terms of breaking information down into threes, I've tried to practise what I preach in this book. There's a lot of information here, so I've broken the core journey of creating a presentation down into three parts that happily make the acronym MAP – Message, Audience, Presenter. It's not the only way of describing how to create a presentation, but it's easy to understand and remember, which means you're more likely to use it.

Within those three sub-categories, I've included many more threes. They're dotted throughout the text – have a look at the lists in this section. I wrote them deliberately as threes, because it makes them easy to understand, easy to remember, and easy to believe. (Sorry!)

Now that you're fully committed to breaking your

message into threes (you are, aren't you?), let's look at the best way to do that.

Three thirds

This section will show you how to divide your next presentation into threes. First, take another look at the structure diagram for your presentation, and remind yourself of your main goal and message.

You're going to break this into three main points. There's a simple way to do this:

SIGNPOST

Write down or say out loud, and complete, the following list.

If you only remember three things from my presentation today, those three things will be:

1.

2.

3.

Trust your instinct with this. If you are already clear on your goal and you've done some work on the hook, this should come easily to you. These three points should be the largest you can think of. They should act as 'mental pegs' to guide you and your audience through your presentation.

Write those three points down, and then jot down all the different bits of information that you want to get into your presentation, putting each one under the appropriate point. Doing this helps you in many ways. It gives a quick, clear structure for your own thoughts. It helps you to spot problems or gaps in your argument. It also gives you the discipline of knowing what to leave out. Presenting is often about the act of content creation, but it's also about the art of editing things out.

Here's a presentation plan based on the MAP process.

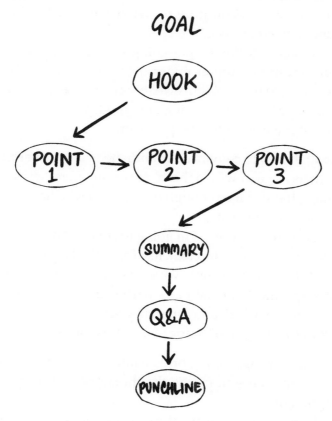

Here are some examples of breaking a presentation into three:

Goal: 'As a result of my presentation, I want my audience to present better.'

Broken into three: 'I'm going to cover the audience, the message, and the presenter.'

Goal: 'As a result of my presentation, I want my audience to agree to fund another full-time staff member, so that we can continue to deliver an outstanding customer experience.'

Broken into three: 'I'm going to cover: 1) why an outstanding customer experience is essential to our business; 2) the problems we're starting to experience because of lack of capacity; and 3) why an extra staff member would solve the problem.'

Goal: 'I need to convince my audience that partnering with us is a win/win for both. As a result of my presentation, there will be enough trust that they're happy to move to the next stage.'

Broken into three: 'I'm going to cover: 1) outcome – what this project could look like for both of us if it's successful; 2) trust – people we've partnered with before and, specifically, what those partnerships looked like, how they worked, and what they say (notice that sublist of three!); 3) next steps to take this forward.'

Almost any topic can be broken into three, and it's easy for an audience to follow the thread of a 'three-part argument'.

I suggest that, for the three main points, you have a visual/anecdote for the first, some solid data for the second, and something that relates it all back to the audience for the third. You don't have to stick to this order, but it's a solid one for putting your argument forward in the best way because it takes the audience on the following journey:

1. Story/Anecdote: 'Emotional buy-in'.

2. Solid data: 'Ah, this doesn't just feel good – there's some real research to this'.

3. Audience relevance: 'Ok, this idea feels right, it's backed up by evidence, and it's right for me'.

In fact, if you get this right it's hard to see how anyone could fail to be persuaded by your presentation!

Story/Anecdote

There's an old saying in sales: 'Facts tell, but stories sell'. From our youngest days we're told stories. Our brains seem hard-wired to remember them.

Some people are reluctant to put stories or anecdotes in their presentations for fear that they'll feel lightweight or childish. I encourage you to use them, though. Everyone you present to watches films and TV. They tell stories to their children, and they'll repeat gossip about people in the office. There isn't a human on the planet who doesn't love a good story.

When you talk in visual, narrative ways you have a much greater chance of affecting people.

Stories are often the most effective way to get emotional buy-in, to be memorable, and to create intrigue and interest in what's coming next. If you watch great speakers, you'll notice that they use stories again and again. Professional speakers only get re-hired if people have remembered, and will take action on, our main points. As a professional presenter, if I don't use stories the chance of my points being remembered drops significantly.

Think of a dull presentation you sat through recently. I'll bet that the presentation was just a collection of facts, with no sense of narrative or story as part of it. You probably had to make a lot of mental effort to understand the points the presenter was making, and you probably didn't feel inspired to take action as a result of the presentation.

NARRATIVE

Think of 'story' in its widest possible sense. I often use the word 'narrative' rather than 'story' as this is closer to what you should aim for in a presentation.

A good narrative for a presentation will involve at least three things: an initial state, a problem or struggle, and a resolution of the problem. In fact, here's the formula for the world's oldest and most successful story:

1. Boy meets girl.
2. Something goes horribly wrong.
3. They resolve the problem and live happily ever after.

It's a great model for structuring any story in your presentation. David Mitchell is one of my favourite novelists, and he said: 'The trick to writing a compelling narrative is so simple I'm surprised it's so often overlooked. Create a character the reader loves and make horrible things happen to them'.[2]

A presentation could begin:

> 'Today, we have an active base of customers, of varying degrees of loyalty. We're reasonably profitable, and the reception to our two latest apps has been positive. But the world is changing fast, and we're certain that we're going to have some serious competition within the next six months. This competition will be aggressively price-focused in the short term and could decrease customer loyalty in the long term.
>
> 'We have three ideas today that we think will make our solution less open to attack from our competitors by differentiating ourselves significantly and taking proactive steps to cement strong customer loyalty before the competition appears.'

You can see that all three steps of the narrative structure are here. It's clear, focused, and credible.

EMPHASISE THE DRAMA

One common mistake I see a lot of presenters make is to present the solution first, and then mention the

---

2. BBC arts website, 19 September 2001.

problem afterwards. This reduces dramatic tension and makes the story less interesting than it should be.

For example:

'Our web optimisation solution reduces the costs involved in getting your data and is almost invisible to end-users. They don't experience any lag between clicking on a web page and seeing the page appear, whereas previously there'd always be a few seconds delay while the upload was routed through our servers.'

Compare that to this:

'Everyone wants web optimisation, they want the data that it brings, and they want to know that the pages they're displaying to their customers are the most effective at getting business. But what's held everyone back so far is the fact that the tech involved was ruining the user's experience.

'People experienced delays between clicking on a link and getting to the page, and they'd often get 'stutters' – moments where the page didn't load properly. So, you'd get your data, but you lost half your visitors in the process. This forced companies to decide: high volume of visitors, but no idea what was working, or fewer visitors, but with valuable data. It's frustrating – a bit like trying to use a self-service checkout in the supermarket. It should work well, but the reality is frustrating!

'We're thrilled to say that we've eliminated

the problem. We've included the technical data as a hand-out, but, in short, we've got rid of the delays and interference. When a visitor comes to your site, they have a seamless, fluid experience, and you get all the data you need to keep the site optimal.'

This is a reworked pitch from one of my clients. Although the second version is longer, can you see that it's much more dramatic?

It follows the 'classic narrative structure' exactly: initial state – problem – resolution of problem. By the time the problem has been clearly stated, you've got people in the room nodding and saying to themselves, 'Yes, this supplier understands us.' There's some humour in the 'self-service checkout' comment too.

Notice that, by stating the problem clearly before providing the solution, the presenter has already positioned themselves as the knowledgeable expert. It's much easier to trust someone who does this, and we're more likely to listen carefully to their solution. By the time you've got to the solution, there's a sense of expectancy. People will pay more attention to it. Psychologically, it 'closes a loop'.

'JUST LIKE YOU'

Stories that talk about someone or something 'just like you' can be powerful. They leverage social proof, and they are easy to remember.

Let's imagine an internal presentation where

someone is pitching to restructure a graduate programme. They're pitching to the leadership team:

> 'In other companies similar to us, we've seen one of two things happen – either they've allowed grad schemes to emerge piecemeal, and they've been cobbled together by whoever's free in HR, or a flawed grad scheme has been put in place too early and has been followed too rigidly.
>
> 'We've also identified where the problem occurs: it's because leadership teams are busy, and grad schemes are often way down the list in terms of priorities.
>
> 'But we've also looked at other companies similar to us who have got a great grad scheme. The impact of that over a decade is remarkable – future leaders can be identified early, talent can be nurtured inexpensively and well, and loyalty to the brand can be encouraged early on.'

Up to this point, no one is talking directly about their own company, but the implication is clear – people 'just like you' have a similar problem to you, so it's worth paying attention to. This is a story-telling device that works particularly well when you have difficult, or provocative, information. It also works well when you have a few 'home truths' to tell everyone!

THE UNFINISHED STORY

This adds creative tension. The idea here is that you open a story but don't tell the ending straight away – you leave it 'unfinished', or unresolved. You can use this technique to make sure that your audience members are keen to pay attention throughout the whole presentation.

For example, you've started a story about the state of the industry so far, and you then say, 'So it's clear there's a problem, and it's clear that the problem is going to become more serious over the next few years. Before we look at some possible answers, let's look at some data that really shows us how serious this problem could be...' You've left a slight feeling of dissatisfaction in your audience's mind.

A great advantage of this technique is that, when you return to the story later, your audience will be more convinced by the story you're telling. Because you've split the story in half, by the time you return to it the story has 'become true' in their minds.

THE STORY WITH A TWIST

As a magician, I love surprises. Among magicians there's a certain kind of magic trick that has what we call a 'kicker ending'. Just when the trick appears to be over, there's an extra magical effect that really takes the audience by surprise. For instance, someone vanishes from a box on stage – amazing. But wait – he then *appears on the balcony*. Take that, doubters! It's always a winner, and most audiences love it.

The same tactic can be applied to stories. Any story that has a twist, kicker, or surprise is likely to be remembered by the audience. If you can add humour to the story, so much the better. A story with a surprise in it is usually a strong way to lead into the 'data' part of your presentation, too.

In magic, there's another technique we use a lot when performing: 'relaxation of attention'. Often, a magician will do something remarkable and then as you're laughing and clapping – just as your attention is relaxing – they'll do a secret move, or do something to set up the next trick. The fact that your attention is relaxed is what allows them to do this.

You can use this idea in your presentation, especially after a 'story twist'. When an audience is intrigued, surprised, or laughing, you can easily switch to the data, and they're likely to be more primed for it.

Data

Although an emotional connection is key in your presentation, data is clearly crucial too. Used well, data can build on the credibility you've already established and can help you to make your point quickly and effectively.

In the structure diagram, I've recommended that you use your data in the middle of the three points, and this is the most reliable way to use it. I strongly recommend that you never *start* with data – always have at least a hook, and try to also include some story or anecdote to really get the audience's attention.

Here's a golden rule about data: Facts and numbers tell you *what*, but they don't tell you *how* and *why*. In other words, they're not motivating in themselves. They can, however, add a huge amount of impact once an audience has *already* become motivated.

It's hard for an audience member to hold many pieces of data in their head unless they're also linked in a narrative, so either try to keep your data to a minimum or add in a narrative flow to make sense of the data.

With any piece of data, ask yourself: 'Is it more effective as a hand-out, or delivered live during the presentation?' It amazes me how often people don't ask this question when putting a presentation together. Everyone reading this book has sat through a presentation where there was so much data that there was no chance of you remembering it, understanding the impact of it, or acting on it. If you ask yourself the 'hand-out' question, you'll usually find that the majority of the data that you have can be placed in a hand-out or follow-up email.

You don't want to clog up your presentation with so many facts that the audience has trouble following your argument. It's much better at the end of your presentation to hear, 'That's really interesting. Can you tell us more about...?' When someone asks that, it's because they're genuinely intrigued and interested in your offering. Their mind has begun to engage with your presentation, and they're beginning to 'fill the gaps' for themselves.

Don't be afraid of mystery!

I've noticed that many presenters seem terrified of the prospect of an audience not having lots of information. In fact, people often say, 'But if the audience has to ask for more information, isn't that a bad presentation?' Almost always the opposite is true.

Of course, you need enough data to make a serious point, but I strongly encourage you to keep it to the minimum needed to make your point. Don't be afraid of leaving some 'gaps' that the audience will find intriguing. Think of the best films and stories you know. How many of them pose some kind of mystery that you as the reader or viewer find so fascinating that you stick with it 'til the end?

Almost all of them! You can do the same thing with your data.

Good data will have the following characteristics:

- It will be clear. Clear enough for your slowest colleague to follow.

- The data will 'build'. Each piece of data will be stronger, clearer or more impactful than the previous one.

- It will be easy to remember.

- It will make your argument stronger.

- It will be easy for *you* to understand and remember. It's astonishing how many presenters get their own data wrong or have to look at a slide to remember it. Always keep in mind that you're not showing data for its own sake – you're doing it to enhance your argument and build your credibility.

- Ideally, it will be data from, or approved by, a third party. The weakest form of data you can use is, 'I've noticed…' The strongest is, 'According to NASA…'

- It will have a logical hierarchy. Compare these two examples:

  'According to research, people use Facebook six hours a day, LinkedIn one hour a day and Twitter two hours a day.'

'According to research, there's a clear winner in terms of online connection. People use LinkedIn one hour a day and Twitter two hours a day, but the winner by far is Facebook with six hours a day.'

It's a very small change, but it makes a huge difference to the memorability and impact of your data.

- It will allow easy comparisons or points to be made from it. When you're able to compare two things, or show that your data is the source of a lot of information, it makes it much more memorable and credible.

- For example:

  'We use Facebook six hours a day, that's at least as long as most people sleep for. In fact, if you add sleep and Facebook together, you've already lost half the day.'

- It will not be overwhelming in its detail. Where possible, you want the 'headline' data. It's nearly always better to keep details in a hand-out in case people have questions about them, unless your audience is *only* there for the data.

- It will be at least a little surprising or have something new in it. If you want your data to stand out, it can't just confirm what the audience already knows. It has to surprise or intrigue them to some extent.

- It will speak to the audience directly. As with everything we've done so far – the goal, the message, the hook – all your data should be relevant to the audience.

- It will be accurate and attributed. It's really easy to blow your credibility if you get the data wrong, use incorrect data, or use phrases such as, 'I think it was IBM who researched...' *You* are the presenter; it's *your* job to know.

- It will be easy to picture. A well-constructed *and simple* graph or pie chart can often make things easier to understand.

Avoid these common mistakes with data:

- Trying to make graphics do all the clarifying work. Design and data go together. If you're relying on a graphic to explain everything, you need to do more work. If your data is already clear, and a graphic is enhancing it, then you're onto a winner. An excellent resource to help you with this is Jon Moon's book *Clarity and Impact.*[3]

- Using data at the start to make your argument. By the time you get to using data, your audience should be half-way to agreeing with you. Data should 'seal the deal'.

- Deliberately using 'dodgy data'. Don't use anything that you're not 100% comfortable with. Data *will* be challenged, so it's important that you know it inside out and that you haven't misrepresented anything. Too many speakers put data on slides and appear to be seeing the data for the first time

---

3. Moon, J (2016) *Clarity and Impact*, London, Oberon Publishing.

as they read it out to the audience. You must be absolutely in control of your data. (This is true for all your material, of course, but for some reason the problem seems to be worse with data.) Remember, people can check anything online in seconds.

- Using the same kind of data over and over. Remember the Rule of Three here. Try to vary the kind of data you use as much as you can. For example, one percentage, one graph, and one comparison. Varying the data helps to maintain interest.

Something for the audience

This is the third of your main points.

I call this 'something for the audience' because after your story/anecdote, and your data, you want to leave your audience being crystal-clear as to why your message is right for *them*.

When I construct my own presentations and work with clients on their presentations, I've found that putting something 100% 'audience relevant' as the last of the three points works best. It's very satisfying for an audience to be able to follow the path of the story, and then believe in the data, and finally be reminded, 'Oh yes, that's *exactly* right for me.'

There's a paradox regarding this part of a presentation: it's the hardest one to write about, because so much will depend on the particular audience and on what's gone before; however, it's also almost always the easiest to work on when preparing the presentation.

My experience is that, by the time you've spent

thirty minutes getting to know your audience, clarifying your goal, and getting a story and the data together, you know so much about what's relevant for the audience that the main problem is usually having too much material for this part.

It's useful to start this third of your presentation with phrases like:

- So what this means for you is...
- Let's look at why this matters to you right now...
- The implications are clear – this is important for you...

The technique of using questions works well here too:

- So, where is this all leading us?
- So, what does this mean for you?
- How does this affect you?

When you use these kinds of phrases and questions, it reminds the audience to 'wake up' slightly and pay particular attention. I often find that simply saying one of those phrases or questions out loud helps me to write this whole section.

So, how might you use this in the real world?

Let's imagine you're a consultancy, and someone has been presenting about the need to understand buyer behaviour in a digital world. They've presented a story or anecdote about a typical buyer journey ten years ago as compared to today. They've presented some memorable, salient data about how people are now researching online and how often the customer knows more than the seller:

> 'So, it's clear that not only has buying behaviour changed – the buyers themselves have changed. Now, what this means for you as the new business team is significant and important. Currently, all of our new business efforts are directed at acquiring leads and "selling" to those leads. But we've just seen that people don't like that approach.
>
> 'The implication is clear: we need to divert time and resources into building credibility – and we need to build credibility where our audience is looking.'

This is brief (often, this third will be the briefest), but it's punchy and to the point. It's also, in this case, a real wake-up call to the audience. Put yourselves in the shoes of the new business team. You've already been hooked at the beginning of the presentation, and you've been convinced by the story, and by the data, that this presentation is about something important. Now, suddenly the message is clear – we need to do something about it.

It's harder to say no to this message than say yes to it – and that's exactly what you want.

Layering the presentation

In the real world, of course, it's rare that you'll only have one piece of information in each of the three 'Point' boxes for your presentation. You might need several stories, quite a bit of data, and a few points of direct relevance for the audience to make your point and be credible.

I recommend that you stick to the three-part structure and 'layer' each point. Sticking to the flow of story–data–relevance works well, even if you're repeating that structure several times.

For example, your first point might have a story, some data, and then a final example to make the point relevant. But make sure that this is all contained under the first point – don't start creating lots of different sub-points, or you risk losing the audience.

Let's say that you're presenting about the importance of trust in building relationships with clients. Your first point might be: 'Outstanding service is the key to ongoing trust.'

In the first box, you'd write 'Outstanding service'. You might then choose to have a couple of stories about how great service has built customer loyalty. You can add some data that links excellent service with commercial results, and then you might want to give an example of where the current audience is doing well (or badly) with customer service. You've used several of the tools, but it's clear to the audience that we're still on point one – this is all about customer service.

Your second point might be: 'But customer service isn't enough to maintain trust from clients. We also need to have more digital offerings – especially apps. Our customers are looking more and more for quick, online answers and products.'

Here, again, you might tell an anecdote about a customer who left your company because your digital products are weak. You might use some data to illustrate how your competitors are taking your clients with their superior apps. And you might ask the audience to consider how difficult it's going to be to retain trust if the business doesn't put significant effort into building some great apps for clients.

You've used several 'layers' here – stories, data, and relevance – but again it's clear to the audience that this whole section is about 'apps' and how they relate to the overall theme of 'trust'.

Layering is an excellent way of getting your message across memorably and helping your audience to act on it. Keeping the layers together and remaining clear about the division into three sections will make the presentation easy to understand and, therefore, more persuasive.

SIGNPOST

Work out what your three sections are going to be. Decide what story, data, and relevant comments you need for each point.

Summary

The summary is usually the easiest part of your presentation, but many people get it wrong.

A lot of people begin, 'So, to summarise…' Beware of what happens in your audience's mind when you do that. They know this means you're near the end of your presentation, and they often start mentally leaving the room or checking their diaries to see what's coming next. You can easily lose the audience at this point.

It's also a mistake to use your summary as an excuse to repeat everything you've just said, but faster. If you've hooked your audience and broken your message into threes, you don't need to do this. It's appropriate to repeat your main points – but not in exactly the same way. Ideally, your summary will provoke the audience to further, deeper thought.

Your summary is an excellent opportunity to remind the audience of either your overarching goal or your main point. It's a chance to bring your three main points together in a way that the audience can easily grasp. It's a moment where you can clarify for the audience what your message means to them, and what action they might need to take.

You don't always need a summary, and when you do have one I recommend keeping it as brief as possible. Your three main points should be strong enough to make the argument you wish to make without one. Think of your summary as a tool for extra clarity, rather than just repetition.

Here are three reliable techniques for your summary:

1. **Remind your audience of your main goal or message.** For example: 'So the message from my presentation today is simple. I want you to have the knowledge you need to get your teams on board with this project, and I hope that the last thirty minutes have been useful...'

2. **Sum up without using the word 'summary'.** You might, for instance, say: 'Everything I've said today leads to one conclusion…'

3. **Let the audience know that there's plenty more information after the presentation if they need it** (see the 'Slides or hand-outs?' section of Chapter Four). For example: 'Obviously, in our brief time, I've only been able to cover the main points. I've got lots of background information in this hand-out that I'll give you at the end…'

Whichever technique you adopt, don't linger on it. Move to questions fairly swiftly. The point of the summary is not to give the audience new information; it's to make sure that your message is clear. See the Chapter Three section titled 'Any questions?' for handling questions well.

Remember also that the summary is not the end of your presentation. You've still got a punchline coming up…

Always have a punchline

The weakest part of most presentations is the ending. Think of what happens at the end of most presentations that you've seen:

- Ok, so that's the presentation. Er… any questions?
- Right, so I think that covers everything… um… Thank you for your time.
- Er… I think that's the end… Oh no, I forgot to tell you…

The last couple of minutes contain so many opportunities that it's almost criminal to waste them like this.

The end of your presentation is your last chance to affect the audience – to hammer home your message, to emphasise your goal, to inspire the audience to take action. Your last chance to leave them feeling confident in your proposal. To give them a simple message they can take away with them and repeat to others.

That's why I call this part 'the punchline'.

Don't think of your ending as a 'summary' or 'wrapping up' – you'll take the life and energy out of it. Thinking of a 'punchline' helps you to remember that there should be a clear and dynamic finish to your presentation.

You'll notice in the structure diagram that I've recommended that you take questions *before* you get to your punchline. You can't always do this, because it depends on the level of formality in the room, but wherever possible I always try to finish with something like this:

'I have one final thought for you to take away, but before that are there any questions?'

It's an elegant and simple way of signalling that you're coming to the end of your presentation, but you still give the audience the opportunity to ask the things that are on their minds.

Taking questions at this point means that your final punchline won't be diluted by audience questions afterwards. You'll be leaving them with *your* message in their minds.

HOW TO CREATE A GREAT PUNCHLINE

You can think of a punchline as the mirror-image of your hook at the beginning of your presentation, and many punchlines refer back to the hook or answer a question that the hook posed.

Many of the techniques that are useful for the hook apply to your punchline as well, so they can be repeated:

- Ending on a thought-provoking quotation;
- Referring back to the beginning of the presentation and adding an extra bit of information or motivation to 'close the loop' in the audience's mind and inspire them to action;
- Using a strong visual aid;
- Using a powerful metaphor, short story, or image;
- Finishing with a question for the audience to take away and think about.

You can also add these sure-fire elements to guarantee a good punchline:

- Let the audience know where to go for additional resources (contacts, websites, further reading, etc;)
- Remind the audience of what they've got from your presentation;
- Remind the audience why the presentation is relevant *for them*;
- And – thank them for their attention and wish them well with the rest of their day (I know it sounds simple, but so many people forget!).

It's also worth double-checking your main goal, to see whether you're still keeping to that. It's very easy to lose sight of your main goal as you're preparing a presentation.

A good punchline will have the following characteristics:

- It will be easy to remember.
- It will be brief.
- It will be easy for people to repeat it to other people who weren't at the presentation.
- It will move people to action, or inspire them to think differently.
- It will be well rehearsed.
- It will be confident and clear.
- It will 'close' the presentation.
- It will reinforce your goal.
- It will reference the audience – leading on from the 'audience relevant' part of your presentation.

But there are also punchline mistakes to avoid:

- Making it up on the spur of the moment (this happens more than half the time).
- Simply repeating what you've already said.
- Losing confidence and asking for questions after your punchline.
- Reading the ending from the slide.
- Introducing an entirely new idea.
- Apologising for not being able to cover everything:

it's your presentation, and you are in charge of time-keeping.

Here's an example of an excellent punchline from someone whose goal was, 'To get increased resources to go out to campuses and attract talented undergraduates early on, so that they are really keen to work with us by the time they graduate.'

She'd delivered an excellent presentation, the audience were hooked, and she made a compelling and intelligent argument for the importance of influencing graduates early. She'd also spelt out the importance of meeting graduates within a certain time frame, since this was when they were most curious about employers.

She knew that, although people in the room would be likely to agree with her, the internal wheels turned very slowly, and she really wanted her punchline to energise people and force them to take action soon; so her punchline went like this:

'I think we all agree that attracting undergraduates early on is important. In fact, it's crucial. The success of this business in twenty years' time will depend on the recruitment activity that we take today. But this can't just be an idea, this has to be something that we take action on.

'For every 200 students, there will only be one that's right for us. In every academic year, there's only one chance to make that first contact count. But think about this – it's easy to believe that if we don't reach that student this time then there will be other opportunities, but this is false.

'Even as we've sat here today, other employers have made plans to reach that student. They
know what he or she looks like. They know when
to contact them. They know how to contact
them.

'This September, dozens of employers will be
heading for that same student, and they will
be doing it well. If they succeed, then not only
do we lose that student but we lose the "buzz",
the word of mouth that successful students can
spread about great employers.

'Fundamentally, this isn't about "graduate
recruitment" – this is about the future of our
business. So I'd like to leave you with a question:
"Can we afford the luxury of inertia when what
we're really talking about is the future of our
business – shouldn't we act immediately?"'

I hope you can see how riveting this is for a certain type of audience and how clearly it finishes the
presentation. What my client had also done, of course,
is finish with this clever idea of making sure that
the importance of graduate recruitment had been
reframed as something crucial for everyone in the
room. At the end of this presentation it's hard to disagree with her conclusion. And if you can't disagree
with her conclusion, you have to agree to take action!

I had a debrief with my client after this presentation,
and it was a great pleasure to hear her talk about the
results of it:

'I was aware that, culturally, people paid lip-service
to recruitment. We were basically seen as an

unimportant sub-department of HR, and we had a weird entanglement with marketing too.

'Over a series of presentations like this, I was able to raise both the profile and importance of graduate recruitment within the business and start to get some serious commitment from senior stakeholders. Interestingly, this also meant that people began to take graduates more seriously and expect more of them. In turn, this meant we were able to get more funding for internal training, and ultimately more buy-in for early campus efforts, since it became obvious to everyone that the better the initial quality of the graduate the easier it would be to work with them and to train them.'

She was thrilled with this result, and so was I. It validated the idea of making sure that people take action by using a clear punchline. It also validated the claim earlier in this book that people who present well become known as experts in their business. They transcend their job titles and become trusted advisors.

SIGNPOST

Decide on the punchline for your next presentation. What do you want the audience to do, or believe, at the end of your presentation?

Repeat, repeat, repeat

How do you make sure your message is memorable? The answer is simple – repeat everything. Repeat everything. Repeat. Everything. (Sorry, I can't help myself!) Repeat. Repeat. Repeat.

I'll repeat something I've mentioned several times already in this book: you must repeat your key messages. It's no accident that I'm doing this in the chapter on repetition.

It's a strange quirk of the human mind that we tend to believe things more if we understand them quickly and can remember them. The advertising industry is built almost entirely on this model, creating simple, clear messages that are easy to recall: 'Beanz Meanz Heinz', 'Because I'm worth it', 'Have a break, have a KitKat'. Advertisers spend millions creating and delivering these simple messages because they stick.

If you stop to think about it for a moment, it isn't rational or fair that we should believe memorable messages more. After all, some of the most credible, well-researched ideas on the planet are incredibly difficult to remember (I've spent years trying to understand physics, and I can't even remember the bits that I used to understand!).

But great presenting is not fair, and audiences are not rational. To repeat the point again: presenting is all about how you *affect* an audience with information. One of the surest ways to make an audience remember your point, and therefore believe it, is to repeat it.

Think over the last few unconvincing presentations you saw. It's almost certain that the presenter did not repeat their points enough. They probably laid out a stream of information – Point A, followed by Point B, etc.

Great presenters don't do this. They make their points as clearly and simply as they can, and they repeat them often. Of course, they don't do it clumsily; they'll usually repeat the same point in different ways – once through a story, then through a catchphrase, then by reminding the audience of the main point in the story, for example. Very occasionally, repeating exactly the same phrase several times throughout the presentation can be effective, but it's usually safer to change the way the point is repeated.

If you follow the 'Busy Person's Structure' then you will be automatically repeating your main points at least three times. It always pays to check, however.

PRIMACY AND RECENCY

There's a strange phenomenon from the world of psychology described as 'the primacy and recency effect'. Several studies have been conducted on this effect, and the format is roughly the same in each one: participants are shown a series of words, one after the other, and are asked to recall them. Typically, people will recall more words from the beginning of the list and the end of the list than from the middle.[4]

There's some controversy over the meaning of these

---

4. Ebbinghaus, H (1913) *On Memory: A Contribution to Experimental Psychology*, New York, Teachers College.
   Murdock, BB (1962) 'The serial position effect of free recall', *Journal of Experimental Psychology*, 64(5), 482–488.

experiments, and obviously people sitting in a lab being asked to recall things is very different to the situation most of your audiences will be in.

However, from my own experience, and that of hundreds of clients, I have no doubt that the primacy–recency effect is important in presenting. There are two reasons why it's useful for you to bear it in mind:

Firstly, make sure that your most important points are mentioned, in some form, near the beginning of your presentation and repeated near the end – ideally in a form that is easy to remember, like a slogan, short phrase, or image.

Secondly, canny presenters give themselves lots of moments of 'primacy and recency'. How do they do this? They deliberately place 'peaks and troughs' in their presentation. They give their presentation a sort of 'ebb and flow' so that there are more possibilities for moments of primacy and recency.

There are many ways to do this. Asking the audience questions, passing out a hand-out, introducing another speaker, introducing a product or prop, getting the audience involved in an interactive exercise – such as a quiz, test, or quick discussion – or changing style – such as from a story to data.

When you put several moments of change in your presentation, you give the audience a much greater chance of remembering your material. It's really in your own interest to do this – remember, the more the audience can remember your presentation the more they'll believe it!

How a ham pie can make your message persuasive

You've now come a long way with your presentation. You know what your core message is, and you've structured that message for maximum impact and clarity.

Sometimes, though, it's possible to forget that your presentation is nearly always an attempt to persuade people of something, and so this section will help you to ensure that your presentation is persuasive.

- Which do you think is healthier for you – broccoli or chocolate? Broccoli, right?

- Second question: which do you eat more often – broccoli or chocolate?

Whenever I talk to audiences about becoming more persuasive I ask the above two questions. Audiences are almost unanimous on the first question – broccoli is healthier for you than chocolate.

Every time I ask the second question, people start laughing. Why? Because almost everyone eats chocolate more often than they eat broccoli. Yet, they've just agreed that broccoli is healthier than chocolate and, therefore, they should eat broccoli more often.

There's a profound, useful, and important truth

behind these simple questions – we make emotional decisions as often as we make rational ones, and once we've made an emotional decision we stick to it like glue:

'Well, I *know* I should eat broccoli more often, but chocolate *tastes* so lovely!'

The implications of this should inform every part of your presentation – once someone has made an emotional decision, the astonishing ability of the human mind to believe anything kicks in, and it becomes almost impossible to change people's minds.

Data alone is clearly not the best way to persuade and engage people, and yet this is how almost everyone presents – they parade a series of facts and hope that facts themselves will convince. But facts, alone, are unpersuasive. They're not motivating, rarely engaging, and almost never memorable.

Instead of using just facts, think of H-A-M P-I-E. These six letters contain almost everything you need to know to persuade people with your presentation.

HAM

HAM stands for: Hearts And Minds.

In most business presentations people make the mistake of going for the minds first – they present 'facts', statistics, numbers, data, etc.

But, as we've seen in the example above, unless there's emotional buy-in *first*, facts are an unreliable tactic.

It's fair to say that in presenting there's no such

thing as a 'fact' – there's only information, which an audience will be more or less inclined to believe and act on depending on the emotional decisions they've already made:

- Do they like you?

- Does your message sound credible?

- Is this worth their time?

- Does this sound relevant?

- Is it interesting?

- Will I be better off, or more respected, or better informed, after hearing this?

All of these sorts of questions can be running through an audience member's mind, and certainly on an emotional level they'll need an answer to these *before* you start throwing your major facts at them.

HAM – Hearts And Minds – means that you *must* engage people emotionally before you go for their minds.

'Emotions' in this case isn't about dramatics, hysterics, or tears. It is about getting the audience into a state where they are emotionally ready to listen to your message.

Often when working with clients I'll say to them, 'The audience isn't ready to hear this level of detail yet – you haven't engaged our interest enough.' That's why 'the hook' is a separate part of the structure of a good presentation, and why it's such an important part. Until you've hooked your audience, your facts won't work well for you.

Here is the start of a sales presentation that I was asked to help with. Names and solutions are changed for obvious and comic effect. As far as I know, 'Auto-Present' software doesn't exist, although someone will probably have invented it by the time you read this.

> 'Good morning everyone. This morning we're going to take you through the features of our new AutoPresent software. AutoPresent is not only the fastest solution to presenting needs on the market, its unique features and best-in-class functionality mean that it solves most presenting problems easily and simply. It has double the storage space of our previous version and can create 500 presentations per minute. It also features duplo-presenting, meaning that it can run two presentations back to back one after another. It also potentially saves money...'

Now, this isn't a *terrible* start to a presentation, but it's forgettable and unmotivating. Look over it again and see how many facts there are, and notice how few of those facts actually *mean* anything to the audience yet. 'It's the fastest solution...' Well, so what? Maybe I don't need a faster solution. Maybe my problem isn't speed at all.

Look, now, at what happened after we worked with the idea of HAM to create a different opening:

> 'Good morning, everyone. As you know, we've been talking to lots of your people internally about your presentation needs. We've collected the responses, and this is what we've uncovered:

'Presentations are really important to your business. Much more important than many of your colleagues realise. In fact, last year over two thirds of your new clients came to you because of a presentation.

'Not only that, but clients who come to you because of a presentation are a dream to work with. They're already "sold", not only on your solutions but also on the idea of working with you as a company. You've noticed that they tend to be more loyal, and they also refer you more often.

'There's something else – compared to advertising and sales efforts, presentations are extremely low cost for you.

'It seems the only question is: "Why aren't we doing more presentations, more often?"

'We've asked exactly that question – both to your people and to nearly ninety other clients over the last three years, and each time people say the same things:

"It takes ages to put a presentation together."

"I'm not confident at going out to present alone. I hide behind sending an email instead."

"Our teams are a mixture of talent levels, so we're not consistent."

'It's these problems, and others like them, which are holding you back in terms of successfully acquiring new clients through your product presentations.

'Because we kept coming across similar problems, we created AutoPresent...'

These two beginnings are profoundly different.

The first is a list of facts – there's no emotional engagement for them at all. The first presentation is forgettable, uninteresting, and easy for a competitor to beat.

The second is so different that it begins to challenge the idea of what a presentation is. The presenter frames the entire presentation from the point of view of the audience. She reminds them not only of the problems they're facing but also of what their company could potentially be like if they solved these problems.

She builds the problems, cleverly throwing in some serious credibility (she mentions ninety other clients), and makes sure that the minds of everyone in the room are focused where she wants them to be.

Until the last sentence, there's no mention of her product or service. She waits until she's got the emotional engagement first. Of course, now she will start to use 'facts' – she can introduce the various features and benefits of her system. But the way the audience will hear these facts is entirely different, because they now know what the facts *mean* to them.

Every single client I've ever worked with has benefited by working with HAM, and if you only take one idea from this book it should be this one. Ask yourself the question: 'Am I engaging people emotionally before presenting the facts? Are they *really* ready for my message?'

PIE

PIE stands for: Pictures, Interest, and Enthusiasm.

Pictures. I'm referring to 'pictures' in their broadest sense – metaphor, analogy, narrative, imagery, and so on. I couldn't include all the words in the acronym because it would have become HAM PIMANIIE, which would have been insane, so 'pictures' will have to do.

The 'Story/Anecdote' section of this chapter contains most of what you need to know to craft a good image, but the basic idea here is that you're more likely to make an emotional connection if you speak to the visual parts of your audience's brains.

Painting a verbal picture is often a successful tactic for engaging an audience because most of us think visually – we mentally picture a successful outcome or happier future, and we find visual messages easy to understand, easy to remember, and easy to relate to. Great presenters fill their presentations with phrases such as, 'Imagine if...', 'What would it be like if...', and 'Picture the scene...'

Interest is so obvious that it shouldn't need stating. Time and again I've seen presenters talk about what matters to *them*, not considering whether it's at least as interesting to the audience.

The problem stems largely from the fact that we're all busy. When we're busy, we leap for easy solutions. In the case of presenting, easy solutions come in two forms – 'Use PowerPoint' and 'Just list all the information I have available'.

The structure I've given you in this book will help you cure this problem by keeping you focused on your audience while preparing and delivering your message. However, there's one quick tip that a lot of clients find especially useful:

When you've got your presentation almost ready, ask yourself this simple question: 'Is what I'm about to present at least as interesting to my audience as it is to me?' It sounds really simple, but when I ask my clients to do it at least half of them start looking like guilty six-year-olds as they realise that they were about to embark on 'their stuff', rather than 'what their stuff *means* to an audience'.

One of the hardest things that any human can do is see the world through other people's eyes and make a serious attempt to understand a message from another person's point of view. If you can do this, your message will be much more persuasive.

Enthusiasm: this is probably my favourite word in the English language. You have to be enthusiastic about your own message if you expect other people to be persuaded by it. You have to persuade yourself first.

Audiences are amazingly intuitive. As an audience, we *know* when someone genuinely believes their own message and when they don't. In your presentation, you have to find the things that you're enthusiastic about, and you have to find the things that your audience should be enthusiastic about.

The original meaning of the word 'enthusiasm' was 'inspired by a god'. You don't have to go that far, but I like the idea that you're inspired by something – the presentation isn't about *you*, it's about the message.

I've chosen the word 'enthusiasm' deliberately (not just because it fits the acronym!). People often mention 'passion' when talking about presenting, but 'passion' is not the best word to use for what you need in a business presentation.

I was once in a room of six people gathered to watch some presentations. The first person gave a decent presentation. Then the second person stood up, walked to the end of the (small) room, and, in a loud, strained voice, started talking at us – passionately. Not *to* us – *at* us. Passionately. And loudly. He looked over our heads with passion and appeared to be passionately talking to the far wall. Lots of passionate arm waving. Passion. Lots of it.

It wasn't comfortable for anyone. More importantly, though, his 'passion' prevented him from getting his message across. We were so distracted by the performance that we couldn't focus on what he was saying, despite the fact that his presentation seemed never-ending.

Enthusiasm is different. It's not about talking loudly and quickly or waving your arms about. It's about being committed to a message, knowing the message inside out, and knowing that the message is right for your audience. True enthusiasm is infectious, and it builds credibility. Audiences relate to a presenter's enthusiasm, and they enjoy it.

It's worth taking a few minutes to go over your presentation before delivering it and to ask yourself: 'What am I most enthusiastic about?' and 'What should my audience be enthusiastic about?'

And that's it for this section. In terms of putting together a persuasive message, HAM PIE will give you a lot of sustenance!

SIGNPOST

Use HAM PIE for your next presentation. Ask yourself:

- *Why* should the audience listen to what I have to say?
- Is my presentation all data, or have I engaged the audience emotionally? Is the data strong enough to support my message?
- Are there any pictures, analogies, or stories I could use to support my message?
- Is my presentation genuinely interesting to my audience – does it answer *their* needs, worries, and wants?
- Am I enthusiastic? Do I believe in what I'm going to present?

CHAPTER TWO
The Audience

Nobody is interested in you

I received an email, late one Tuesday evening, from someone who'd been recommended to me. He had an important presentation coming up and desperately needed help.

The last sentence of his email will stay in my memory forever: 'Please help. I've got the charisma of a camel.'

So, we met, and I asked him to show me his presentation. He was a finance director but presented rarely and clearly hated every minute of it. His presentation was, as you've probably guessed, pretty dreadful. I asked him to talk me through how he prepared it. He began with, 'Oh, well, I get my assistant to sort some slides out for me...'

'No,' I interrupted. 'Right from the moment you

know you're going to have to present. What's the first thing you focus on?'

'Oh,' he replied. 'Well, erm, I think I probably start worrying. Well, I start thinking about what I'm going to say, and how I'm going to fill the forty-five minutes.'

And there, of course, lay the root of the problem. He started off by thinking about himself rather than the needs of his audience. And almost everyone does this. Don't do it. It's bonkers.

I hear these phrases over and over again: 'I need to get my slides ready first', 'I need to talk about X, Y, and Z', 'I need to speak for forty-five minutes', 'I need to look confident'.

These phrases reveal that the presenter has begun by thinking about themselves first. But when you do this, you're really putting the cart before the horse.

The title of this chapter tells a fundamental truth – *nobody is interested in you*. This sounds like a harsh statement, but remembering this will help you focus and give your presentation energy. Every audience member is listening to your presentation and thinking, 'What's in this for me?' If you can answer that question, you'll have a Busy Person's quick solution to a great presentation.

Every presentation I've ever given, and every presentation I've ever coached, has improved by focusing on *the audience*.

You're almost certainly an intelligent person. (In fact, you must be – you bought this book. You're probably also extremely attractive and emotionally stable.)

You know that you *should* focus on the audience, but everyone seems to get this part wrong.

So, the first step is to make the decision:

'I will focus on my audience throughout my presentation.'

There are lots of benefits to doing this – the better you know your audience the more precise your message becomes, and the more likely it is that you'll find lots of things to 'hook' them with.

When I present, I always spend some time with the person who's booked me getting to know about the audience. For larger conferences and events, I'll meet some of the audience and get to know them, and their challenges, as well as I can. I always make sure that I can make at least one 'in-joke' during the presentation. It doesn't have to be funny, it just has to say, 'This presentation is especially for *you*; it's not generic.'

Over watching, and giving, thousands of presentations, I've learnt that there are several things you need to know about an audience to make sure that your presentation is going to be dead right for them. We'll go through them in detail here, and they're also written as a checklist at the end of this chapter.

How to get into your audiences' heads

The best way to get into your audiences' heads is to ask questions. Sometimes to them, and sometimes about them.

Below are the questions I use all the time. There's

a more comprehensive checklist at the end of this chapter.

HOW MANY PEOPLE WILL BE THERE?

Presenting to a small number of people is profoundly different from presenting to a large group. (Can you imagine one of Apple's product launches given to a room of three people? It would be ridiculous. The presentations themselves are terrific, but *only* because they're terrific for a certain audience.)

I have a rule of thumb that for every ten people in my audience the entire audience gets slightly slower, and I need to be slightly clearer. When you're speaking to two people, you can speak quickly, you can present lots of ideas, and you can easily lead into a conversation. When you're presenting to 200 people, you need to present with a clear, slow rhythm, and you can only present a small number of ideas with clarity.

WHAT TIME OF DAY WILL IT BE?

Presentations given at different times of the day need to have different 'tones'. If you're presenting early in the morning, people tend to have longer attention spans, and they'll (weirdly) be a bit more rational. If you're presenting early afternoon, it's the 'graveyard shift' where a carbohydrate lull can easily kick in, so you'll need to be prepared for that and have ways of lifting the energy and engaging attention.

If you're presenting in the late afternoon, people's attention spans wander very quickly, so you'll need to ensure that you've got a few 'attention hooks' at various moments during your presentation. If you're presenting in the evening, you can be much 'lighter' in your content, and a little more comical or tongue-in-cheek, depending on your style.

HOW LONG HAVE YOU GOT?

You need to know this – not so that you can 'fill the time' (in fact, I recommend that you don't), but so that you know what the audience's expectations are. I usually subtract 30% from the allotted time. So, if I'm booked in someone's diary from 12.00–13.00, I know we won't start until 12.10 as they'll arrive a bit late. There will almost certainly be another appointment in their diary at 13.00, so they'll probably start 'mind-wandering' at about 12.50, getting ready for their next appointment.

That means I've got a maximum of forty minutes for my presentation and questions.

AUDIENCE DEMOGRAPHICS (BE POLITICALLY INCORRECT!)

You'll make your own judgements about how you change your material based on different audience types, but you may need to know the answer to the following questions:

What's prompted this presentation? What's the back-story? If the demand for the presentation has come from another person, department, or company, you need to be clear about what their needs are because the only reason they're asking you to present is to try and get those needs met. If you're not clear enough about what those needs are, you can't meet them.

If the need for the presentation has come from you (in other words, if you've invited people to come to your presentation), then you need to make sure that the audience knows what *you* think the backstory is, otherwise they won't know in what context to see your presentation.

I've learnt this lesson through (slightly) painful experience. I give a presentation on how to become more persuasive and influential. I used to start by just talking about some really useful persuasion techniques, but I soon realised that I wasn't giving the audience enough context. I needed to start by saying, 'The skills are useful in terms of new business development,' or leadership skills, or getting internal buy-in. Giving the audience this context makes it much easier for them to relate to the material.

Once I realised that my audience needed more context, my presentation quickly became much clearer.

What problems are your audience hoping to solve? Audiences are not empty vessels waiting patiently for your fascinating information. They bring with them a mental agenda, and this is often based on wanting you to solve a problem for them or clarify something for them. If you're clear on this, and speak to it, your audience will love you. Think, 'What's in this for me?'

What's the educational level of the audience? This will affect how you organise and deliver your content, and what you choose to emphasise. This question covers industry knowledge as much as academic qualifications.

What's the age range of the audience? It's useful to know this, particularly if you tend to add references to music or other popular culture in your presentations.

What are the levels of seniority in the audience? This is an essential question to consider, for several reasons. Firstly, if you're trying to speak to the needs of your entire audience you'll need to know whether they're all at a similar level of seniority or whether to vary your content to include everyone.

It's also important because of the possibility of questions and interruptions. When there's a wide mixture of levels of seniority, then sometimes the more senior people in the room will try and assert their seniority by asking trick questions or demonstrating that they 'know this already'.

Sometimes, the reverse can happen – the less senior people can try and demonstrate their importance to the senior people by asking 'clever' questions or demonstrating that they know more than you, the presenter. It's not difficult to handle these questions and interruptions (see the 'Any questions' section in Chapter Three), as long as you know they're likely to be there. If you know the seniority levels of your audience members, it will help you to spot the problem and prepare for it before it arises.

What are the likely objections or obstacles to your message? It's rare that anyone has a message that's right for everyone. Predicting the objections in advance makes it much easier to deal with them. You can either address the objections as part of your message, or you can prepare for them during questions.

Is there a 'second audience'? This is a secret weapon for you. Often – much more often than we might realise – we're not presenting only to the people in the room. We're also presenting to the people that they are going to talk to after the presentation.

For example, in a sales presentation, the team you're presenting to will often have to present their business case to others internally. If you're trying to get internal resources, the people you're presenting to will have to justify their decision to their superiors (and, sometimes, shareholders). If you're presenting to get buy-in to a project, or as part of cultural change, you'll often want your message to be passed on enthusiastically to people who aren't in the room. When you know that your message has to be not only understood by people in the room but also transmitted to others, it forces you to clarify your message and make it as clear and simple as possible.

Often you can tell your audience exactly what you're doing and even give them instructions on how to convey your message. Many of my clients use statements such as:

> 'Obviously, some of you are going to discuss this idea with colleagues, and they'll probably want to know more about timescales for implementation. Well, basically, we've got a really useful project planner here that shows typical timescales and milestones that help to keep the project on track.

We'll leave this as a hand-out at the end, so that you can discuss it, but for now, the essential details are...'

Notice what happens in this case: First, you're acknowledging the world of your audience, in the process demonstrating your credibility. Second, you're asking them to imagine themselves in a particular situation, and they will. They'll immediately bring to mind the people they're going to have to talk to. For some of the audience, this will be a burdensome task, and they'll picture that. *Then* you immediately present them with a solution – we've done the work for you, and we've pre-empted the situation. If you remember that so much of what's going on in presenting is *emotional* as well as rational, you'll see why this is so important.

By the time you've finished presenting that paragraph, you've solved *your* problem – that your message has to be conveyed to a 'second audience' clearly and simply – but you've also solved a problem for the audience that they might not have known they had!

In presenting, this is dynamite – everyone wins, and you've got the audience on your side. You've also set up some reciprocity, which makes the world a better place!

SIGNPOST

There's no such thing as a good presentation. There are only presentations that are *good for a specific audience.*

Don't tell them what they want to hear

Imagine you're about to present a monthly update. You begin, 'So, I'm going to give the monthly update now…' You then give the monthly update and ask for questions.

This is what the audience expect to hear, and this is what they think they want to hear. But the fact that this presentation is so predictable means that it's also likely to be forgettable.

Audiences often find it boring when they're only told what they already know or what they want to hear. It's exciting and interesting for an audience when they're presented with an idea they haven't thought of before, or when you help them see what they do know in a new way.

Look again at the title of this section – 'Don't tell them what they want to hear'. It's deliberately worded to make you think and to get your attention. At least some of your presentation should do the same – make the audience think and get their attention. One of the best ways to do that is to make sure that there's at least one moment where you *don't* tell them what they want to hear.

The busy person's way to do this is to ask themselves the following question: 'What does my audience *expect* to hear and what do they *need* to hear?'

If you can exploit the difference between these two things, you instantly have a more dramatic presentation. For example: 'What you expect to hear me talk about today is the monthly update, but actually what we need to focus on is why nobody pays attention to the monthly update!'

SIGNPOST

Presenting is an ineffective way of giving information. It's expensive to get people together for a presentation, and it takes a lot of time. If you just want to give your audience some information, it's much more effective to email them or send a brochure. Presenting isn't about information, it's about how you affect the audience with your information. Don't tell them what they want to hear – be more interesting than they expect!

Everyone you present to is tired, hungover, or late

Have you ever started daydreaming during a presentation? Or felt a bit sleepy? Or checked your phone to see what your next meeting is fifteen minutes before the end of the current one?

It's OK, I won't tell anyone. We all do it.

Bad presenters blame their audiences for doing this. They simply reel off their information and tell people, 'I'll send you the slides.' They don't care if their message affects the audience, they just want to get through the presentation. They say to themselves, 'Well, I did the presentation; it's not my fault if they didn't "get it".'

What an opportunity you miss every time you present like this. You miss the chance to stand out from the crowd, to build your credibility, and to get people to act on your ideas.

Here's the Busy Person's way to avoid being this kind of presenter:

Say to yourself, 'I'm going to present as if my audience is tired, hungover, or late.'

Having this idea at the forefront of your mind will help you to stick to basics and make sure that you are focused on what your audience gets, rather than what you've got to give.

In my coaching sessions with clients, I often ask them to do their presentations to me 'as if I'm hungover and running late in my day'. The difference is immediate – the message becomes more focused, the fat is stripped, and the presenter becomes more energised and convincing. Interestingly, even their body language and levels of energy change. Their commitment to communicating the message is greater. There's a sense of urgency. All of these things make you a more dynamic presenter.

So, remember: as you're preparing for your next presentation, ask yourself, 'How would I present this if my audience were tired, hungover, and in a hurry?' You'll find a surprising difference, and with almost no effort!

How to customise for difference audiences

In every presentation I give about presenting, a member of the audience always asks some version of the following question: 'How do I tailor my presentation when there are different audiences at the same presentation?' Here's an example:

'I have a problem. I run a global team, and we run a teleconference presentation every two weeks. About half of my team are based in Japan, and half in the United States. It's important that I get through all of the information with my team, and that I hear all of the questions and challenges my team have. But the Americans tend to interrupt a lot – they'll ask questions all the way through, and often that means I don't get all my information out. But worse – the Japanese hardly say anything, and they almost never question me. I'm their boss, and they have a terror of either looking wrong or disrespecting me. How do I deal with this?'

This was the problem presented by Andrew, a client of mine, and it's a tough one.

It's important to remember that you're *always* tailoring your presentation to your audience. The only thing you need to decide is whether you're going to do this accidentally, during the presentation, or consciously when you're preparing. It should be obvious which option is the best. The only extra complication that Andrew has is that he is dealing with different types of audiences in the same presentation.

One of the key messages of this book is that everything in your presentations will be improved if you prepare well, and this lesson is particularly true here. Taking some time to understand the different needs of different audience members will pay dividends in the presentation itself.

In the example above, Andrew has two problems – the problem of the audience and the problem of the technology he's using to engage with them. See 'Online presentations' in Chapter Five for a detailed discussion of how to present using online tools and phones, but for now let's look at how to deal with different types of audiences.

In this example, it's obvious that Andrew has to get several things right. He has to present extremely clearly and precisely, so that his message will land with both of his audiences, even when he's not physically present. He has to make sure that his audience gets what they need, but also that he achieves his own goals. He has to keep his team functioning, despite their differences.

I encouraged him to follow the MAP process and focus firstly on the question, 'What do I want my audience to *do* as a result of my presentation?'

It was obvious that one of the things he wanted his audience to do was to ask questions and get involved. The problem was that half his audience was doing that too much, so he needed to tone them down, while encouraging the other half to get more involved.

We looked at various ways of achieving his goal while also making sure that the audience got what they wanted from the presentation. After a few minutes of discussion, Andrew decided to present in the following way:

In the 'hook', he'd let the audience know that he wanted them to get maximum value from each presentation, and to do that he needed to establish a couple of guidelines.

He told the audience that he would be presenting in roughly six-minute segments, with one idea, suggestion, or update every six minutes. At the end of each six-minute segment, he would stop and take at least one, but not more than three, questions from each team. If there were no questions he'd move on, but there would be no time to go back at the end of the presentation and ask questions about earlier segments.

He tried this approach and it worked like a charm. The Japanese team members knew that they would be expected to ask at least one question at the end of each segment, and if they didn't they'd lose the opportunity, and this gentle pressure forced them to get involved. On the other hand, the American team members could *just about* wait six minutes without interrupting (don't hate me if you're American – you know it's true). By paying attention to both the needs of the audience and his own goal, Andrew was able to customise his presentation for audiences that were culturally very different, leaving everyone happy.

As a delightful footnote to this story, I worked with Andrew on several other projects, and about six months into this new style of presenting he was happy to tell me that he'd been able to relax the strict guidelines in his presentations because 'my team are working better together than ever before. They are listening to each other much more these days, and they've got to know each other online much better.' In this case, being a good presenter made Andrew a better team leader too.

Here's the big lesson of this section: you're going to have to deal with your audience at some point. If you don't take a few moments to prepare then you'll end up improvising when you're in front of your audience, which is the worst time!

It's much better to try to be clear about the audience *before* you're presenting. Then you get the chance to spot the problems and, where possible, solve them. Being aware that there might be different types of audiences is the first step to dealing with them. If you don't find that out in advance, you definitely can't do anything about it.

Once you've identified the different kinds of audiences, make sure that you've identified what your goal is with each one. For example, let's say that you're a marketing agency and you're pitching a new proposal to an existing client. Part of your proposal involves a considerable investment in new technology. You've identified that the audience will consist of the client's marketing team, plus the finance director, someone from IT, and a new director at the client organisation you've never met before.

It should be immediately apparent that different members of this audience will have different interests, questions, and needs, and that you'll need to tailor parts of your presentation specifically for each. This works in your favour. Audiences love being told that there are parts of a presentation especially for them, and I encourage my clients to be upfront about that. Counter-intuitively, audience members like knowing that they are allowed to 'tune out' of some parts of a presentation.

In the example above, the marketing agency might stress the agenda early on and say:

'Firstly, we'll look at your customers and why this new technology is essential for you to continue to retain and attract customers. Then we'll cover the details of the budget needs and the expected return over the next forty-eight months. Lastly, we'd like to briefly cover some of the technical aspects of implementation. We've scheduled some time at the end for questions...'

You can hear how each of those agenda items is tailored to a different member of the audience – 'your customers and why...' is directed at the marketing team (and the new director, since this is the chance to impress her with your credibility), 'budget' is for the finance director, and 'technical aspects' is aimed at the IT person.

Notice how if you're the IT person you know right from the start that you don't need to give the whole presentation your attention. You can mentally relax a bit, knowing that what's relevant to you is near the end.

If you're the finance director, you need to understand something about the project but your main focus will be on the budget part, and you know that you can 'tune out' after that (unless you're particularly fascinated by IT implementation).

Using the audience checklist at the end of this section will help you to identify the different types of audiences you'll have to present to and make sure that you have something prepared for each of them. They'll thank you for it, and you'll be more prepared and confident.

> **SIGNPOST**
>
> Make sure that you take a moment to identify the different types of audiences for your presentations. Once you've identified them, it's usually fairly easy to make sure that your presentation covers all the different needs of the audiences. Use the checklist at the end of this chapter.

Peaks and troughs

If you're asked to pay attention to anything, the chances are that your attention goes in peaks and troughs. Even watching a gripping drama at home, I expect that you sometimes chat to your beloved/partner/significant other/polyamorous quintet during the programme. Perhaps you pause it for a moment, or you occasionally look at your phone.

Humans are very bad at sitting still and paying attention for long periods of time. Our attention fades in and out, especially if the presenter is not particularly dynamic or engaging. This happens in most presentations, and the longer the presentation the more likely it is that your audience's attention will come and go.

Here's the Busy Person's way to deal with this. Don't fight the natural rhythm of human attention – deliberately build 'peaks and troughs' into your presentation.

There are many ways to do this, and here are some of the most effective:

Vary your vocal delivery. When you rehearse, plan for some moments of change. Sometimes you need to be calm and clear because you want the audience to hear the facts. At other times you need the audience be emotionally engaged, rather than thinking just of facts, so your vocal delivery should be more forceful and passionate. Think of using pauses, changes of volume and changes of rhythm. Think of a 'gear change' every five minutes or so.

Vary the concentration level. I use this technique a lot. If you've had five minutes of detailed technical explanation, follow with a simple illustration or anecdote that people can understand easily. If you've been showing a lot of visual information, switch to using just words for a minute or so (and vice-versa). Add a quotation or provocative statement every so often, or pause and let the audience think for a couple of seconds. A handy technique is to occasionally move away from your slides and use a flip-chart or some post-it notes stuck to a wall. The extra movement helps to maintain interest.

Get the audience involved. My rule of thumb is that I never want to be talking for more than about fifteen minutes without getting the audience involved somehow – perhaps by inviting questions or giving them a question to consider. You can encourage them to talk among themselves or give them a hand-out, visual, or prop. Perhaps leave some important information out and ask them to get involved in guessing what it is. I once saw a presentation to food suppliers in which the presenter asked, 'There's one foodstuff that never spoils. You can eat it even if it has been on the shelves for thousands of years'. He asked the audience what they thought it was. No one guessed the correct answer (honey, in case you're wondering), but the question made for a dynamic 'peak' about two thirds of the way through his presentation.

Use humour. Laughter wakes people up and encourages a happy feeling in the room, which, in turn, encourages more attention. If you're a naturally humorous person, then use it. If you're not naturally humorous, then write a few humorous moments. Self-deprecating comments work well, as do topical comments about your industry.

Where appropriate, ask the audience to move. Sometimes this can be just asking them to talk briefly to the person next to them, or it may be that you have some documents or samples that you need the audience to look at. Moving the audience builds a natural peak into the presentation. Do make sure you're in control of what happens, though – you need to be clear about when the moving has come to an end.

I recommend that you avoid using technology such as video clips or anything that relies on you being connected to the internet to provide peaks in your presentation. Although video and sound clips can work well, the risk of technology failing is high, and I prefer not to be held hostage by a meeting room's capabilities!

As always, the secret is in the planning. Design a

few peaks and troughs into your presentation, and you'll have a much more engaged audience.

How to prepare for difficult audiences

Every presenter will, at some point, face a difficult audience. Sometimes audiences are deliberately difficult for reasons of their own, and sometimes they are accidentally difficult.

The Busy Person's way to deal with difficult audiences is to prepare in advance so that you're ready to handle the situation. The audience checklist at the end of this section will help you to be prepared for most audiences, but sometimes there will be situations that are more difficult than normal. How do you prepare for those?

There are usually three kinds of particularly difficult audiences:

1. Those who have some kind of agenda against you. This is often because of internal politics or your company's track record.

2. Those who don't want to be there for your presentation but have to be. Often they've been forced to be there for professional reasons.

3. Those who are easily distracted or who become distracted because of phone calls, being in the wrong environment, or noisy distractions or interruptions.

Here's how to deal with them:

With all these types of audiences, it's best to manage expectations clearly from the beginning. Specifically, you need to let difficult audiences know that you understand their needs and that you're on their side, or at least that you've prepared something for them. Remember HAM PIE – you need to make an emotional connection first.

With an audience who may have an agenda against you, acknowledge the problem and build trust.

First, be clear about the nature of their objection to you. If you're a supplier, are you likely to have problems because you're presenting against a strong incumbent? If you're presenting a project update to a hostile new director, can you find out the source of their hostility? I once had to present to a group who'd been given a massive project and very little time to work on it. The director still wanted me to present, but the audience were desperate to start work on their project, so every minute with me seemed wasted to them.

Once you've understood the source of the problem, you must make building trust and credibility part of your goal. A key focus of your presentation must be tailored towards getting the audience to 'soften' their attitude towards you.

In the case of my own presentation, I addressed the problem, and I made sure that at least some of my presentation was aimed specifically at helping them complete their project. I began:

'I know that you're all desperately keen to begin work on the project, and that you feel time is running out. I promise you that several of the ideas we're going to explore together in this presentation will help you to complete your project more quickly and easily than before. And you'll have built greater trust with your client, helping you in the future. If you give your full attention to this presentation today, it will save you loads of time across this, and future, projects.'

Obviously, I would have preferred not to have the problem in the first place, but this way of dealing with it worked well – acknowledge the problem and build trust.

Using testimonials and track records can be effective, especially if the problem is that you're presenting to someone who is new to the business and may not know you yet. The Busy Person's way is to *solve the problem as simply as possible while still achieving their goal*.

With audiences who don't want to be in your presentation the key is making sure that you keep the presentation as brief as possible while still achieving your goal. Put as much as you can into hand-outs, brief people in advance, and leave any details for follow-up or questions. Stick to the barest outline of your points and talk about outcomes and results, rather than spending any time on the history of your proposal, or your processes or methodology.

Be frank with the audience about your awareness that they'd rather be somewhere else, and let them know that you've tailored your presentation to suit them. You don't have to be blunt about this – you can use a statement such as:

'I know that my presentation is not exactly top priority for most of you, so I've kept it as brief as possible and will be covering only the top three updates today. If any of you need to know more, I'm happy to answer questions afterwards, and I have a hand-out with more detailed information on it for you to take away.'

Your audience will thank you and be much less difficult to deal with. You're more likely to achieve your goal, because the audience will resent you less.

Sometimes it's possible to consider splitting the presentation into smaller presentations, each one focused on a particular aspect of your proposal or theme. This can help you to avoid the problem of an audience feeling like they're wasting their time. The audience can select which one of your presentations most speaks to their needs, and they can choose to attend only that one.

Distracted audiences can be difficult to deal with, but ignoring the distraction will nearly always make the situation worse. Ignoring it forces people to pay more attention to it, since they're aware of the distraction but they are also aware of your attempts to ignore it, which creates tension in the audience.

It's usually better to identify the distraction. For example, I was once presenting in a conference room, and the catering staff were noisily setting up the coffee outside the door. There was lots of banging and clanging, and the sound of a tray and cups being dropped. I said, looking at the door where the noise was coming from, 'I don't know who's on after me, but I hope it's not the juggler.'

The joke was funny enough to let the audience laugh, and it relieved the pressure of having to ignore the distraction. The distraction became less distracting.

Sometimes the distractions will be focused on one person, but it's not because the person is trying to disrupt – perhaps they've suddenly had to take a phone call. Again, it's wise not to ignore these distractions. It's better to identify the distraction and invite the person to take the distraction outside. Usually the audience will be grateful to you that you've done this. If it's not appropriate to identify the person, then asking the audience to get involved in an activity can take the pressure off the moment. You can, for example, ask the audience to discuss the most recent point you've made or find some solutions to a problem you've laid out.

Every public speaker at some point comes across audiences that just cannot focus. This can be for many reasons – they may have a shared joke, or they might be excited about something later in the day or angry at something earlier. They might not understand why they're having to listen to you, the aircon might be broken, or perhaps they're just affected by the weather/feng shui/random astrological alignment.

There are three ways of dealing with this audience. Firstly, bring HAM PIE into play early – make sure that, right at the start of your presentation, the audience understands *why* they should pay attention to you. Sell the reward for listening, or the pain for not listening.

Secondly, make sure you emphasise the peaks and

troughs. Some audiences are just restless, so try to provide them with plenty of variety to build the peaks and troughs. Think of interactive activities, props, question-and-answer sessions, and even physical movement – sometimes just getting people to stand up and meet someone new or get a coffee can restore their concentration.

Thirdly – keep it short. It's a strange quirk of many presenters that when they face problems they tend to go on for *longer* or make more effort. I think it's because they believe that the more they talk the more the audience are likely to start listening. In fact, the opposite is true.

If you know that you are going to face a restless, unfocused audience then plan your presentation to be as short and punchy as possible.

If you only find out that the audience is restless when you're about to present, then go back to the structured approach and cut to the chase as quickly as possible – remind yourself of your goal, what your hook is, and what your three main points are. If it helps, just jot them down quickly on a piece of paper to give you a quick map through a shortened version of what you've prepared. Let the audience know *why* they should listen, tell them your three main points, and go straight into questions. If you haven't said enough, they'll question you anyway. You all benefit from this approach – the audience will be delighted with a shorter, punchier presentation than they expected, and you'll usually find that the audience engages more (sometimes after the presentation itself).

The audience checklist

I love checklists. They make life easier and quicker. If you're going to present more than once, then don't reinvent the wheel every time – make a checklist.

This is the checklist that I use for every presentation I give, regardless of whether the presentation is to one person in a coffee shop or an audience of hundreds in a conference venue. You don't need to use every question every time, but you'll find most of them useful most of the time.

- What's the context or history to this presentation?
- How many people will be there?
- Are there any internal politics or issues that I need to be prepared for?
- What will be on the audience's mind *before* my presentation? (Another pitch, a meeting, a stressful journey?)
- What will happen *after* my presentation?
- Do I need to send them anything in advance?
- What problems are they hoping that my presentation will solve?
- What do they expect to hear?
- What do they need to hear?
- What single outcome would benefit them most?
- Do I need to prepare any hand-outs or takeaways?
- Will there be other people not in the room who will be told about my presentation?

- Do I know how I will get their attention?
- Am I clear about why I'm delivering *this* message to *this* audience?
- Is there anything I need to know about the presenting environment?
- Is there anything I need to prepare for the presenting environment?
- Are there different types of audiences for this one presentation? If so, have I catered for all of them?

CHAPTER THREE

The Presenter

Finally, we get to you – the presenter.

This is where most people begin to think about presenting. Too many people think that 'presenting skills' are the most important thing to learn in order to be a great presenter.

As you'll have seen throughout this book, your message and your connection to the audience are what make a great presentation. If your message is right for the right audience, you've done almost all of the work required to be a great presenter. However, once you've reached the stage of having a great message, *then* it's the right time to start thinking of your presenting skills. There's no doubt that even a great message will be enhanced by a great speaker.

In this section, we're going to look at the most important skills required to become a skilful, confident, and charismatic presenter. These are skills that

I teach to clients every day, and they reliably improve people's ability to present well. We'll cover the essential skills:

- How to rehearse.
- How to sound great.
- How to look great.
- How to deliver like an expert.

Learning to deliver like an expert is a practical skill, rather like playing a musical instrument or learning to ride a bike. You'll get a lot more out of this section if you actually try out some of the exercises.

I'm so nervous!

The most common question people ask me in my work is: 'How do you deal with nerves?' You're in good company if presenting makes you nervous. I don't know a single presenter or performer who doesn't get nervous before standing up in front of other people to present or perform. I'm going to give you some Busy Person's tips on how to deal with nerves, but it's important to understand what nerves are, and where they come from. If you understand them you can control them better.

It's almost certain that our nervous feelings when we present come from our ancient 'fight or flight' response to a stressful situation. When our ancestors were being chased, or attacked, it was crucial that they protected themselves and escaped. They needed a massive boost of adrenaline to run fast, they needed heightened concentration to observe any dangers, they needed to breathe less deeply so as not to give themselves away, they needed blood to flow differently to protect the essential organs, and their hands and feet got sweaty and damp, possibly to cool down, or perhaps to get a better grip.

We're lucky – all of us are the descendants of the ancestors who made it. We are the children of the 'ones who got away'. All of us have a great-great-great-grandparent who escaped a dangerous animal.

Nerves are also a way of reminding ourselves that we've separated ourselves from 'the pack'. If you watch any nature documentary, one of the things you'll notice about mammals is that we are very social, and we love being in groups. From grazing gazelles to groups of gorillas, mammals stick together for safety.

When you present, you're deliberately setting yourself apart from the pack. You're encouraging the group to focus on you. A tiny part of your brain is yelling: 'If a predator comes along, you'll be first – get back in the group!'

When you think about nerves like this, you stop viewing them as the enemy. The deep, lizard bits of our brains are brilliant at getting us instantly ready for danger but not so good at distinguishing between a tiger jumping at you and standing up to give a presentation – your body reacts to both in the same way. Hands get sweaty, hearts beat fast, breath tightens, and voices go dry. Understanding this gives you a great foundation for dealing with nerves, and we don't need to reinvent the wheel – we can look at what professional performers do to cope.

Many of my best friends are performers, and we often talk about nerves and performance anxiety. I've also worked with hundreds of clients on dealing with nerves and, of course, I present a lot myself and there's one thing that I've noticed works time and time again: identify the nerves, name them, and remind yourself that the nerves are there to help you, not harm you.

Instead of talking yourself into the problem ('Oh, I'm nervous, I feel terrible, this is going to be horrible, I wish I didn't have to do it...'), you can talk yourself out of it by naming what's occurring in your body ('Oh, that's interesting, my heart is beating fast, well that's probably the adrenaline getting me ready to run from a tiger'). You can do this in your head.

Naming the nerves diminishes their effect on you. It takes the sting out of them. It won't cure them completely, but it helps to make them manageable.

Then, remind yourself that the nerves are natural and are there to help you. I say out loud to myself: 'There probably isn't a tiger in the room!' It makes me smile every time I say it, relaxes me, and helps to give some perspective to the nerves.

A lot of performers also have a 'mini-ritual' before performing or presenting, so in the following section I've provided one for busy people.

The one-minute warm-up

The 'one-minute warm-up' is a way to calm your nerves, increase your charisma, and make your voice sound more confident.

Every good presenter, performer, sportsperson, and speaker has some form of warm-up, for two reasons.

Firstly, *any* kind of ritual is useful to put yourself psychologically 'in the zone'. Secondly, just as sportspeople need to make sure that their muscles and minds are fully prepared for the activity they are about to do, a presenter needs to make sure that their body, mind, and voice are warmed up to deliver their presentation well.

When sprinters run, they are doing something unnatural at the edge of their ability. They also know that lots of people are going to be watching them, so sprinting is stressful. Having a warm-up means that they have a structured system for making sure that they are in the best physical and psychological shape possible for competing. A warm-up removes some of the nerves and means that they are not starting 'from cold'.

It's the same for presenters and speakers. I know from painful experience that the times when I've begun to present without warming up have always been worse than when I do warm up. I take longer to 'get going', I don't make a connection with the audience as well as I could, and I sometimes mix my words up. Even a one-minute warm-up puts me in a much more effective state and makes my presentations much better. These days, I'd never dream of presenting without doing a warm-up.

You can warm up by following these steps.

BODY

It should be obvious, but it's often not: when you present, you don't present with your mind. Your audience can't see or hear your mind, and 100% of your presentation is delivered by your body. So make sure that your body is ready.

First, make sure you're grounded. Allow your weight to be evenly balanced on both feet and, just for a moment, let your arms hang loosely by your sides. Enjoy the sense of easy balance. Most of us spend most of our lives hunched, twisted, and tense, so it's useful to allow some of that tension to drop away just before you present. If it helps, shake your arms a little to let tension fall away.

Then, 'centre' yourself. Centring yourself can make you feel more confident and reduce nerves. Place your feet so that they're level and allow yourself to be balanced. Think of your heels releasing into the floor. Then, slowly, raise your arms out to the sides, until your arms are level with your shoulders. Then, turn your hands palm-up and continue lifting your arms until they are making a 'V' shape above your head. Hold this position for a moment.

Make sure that your shoulders and neck aren't tense, and then slowly let your arms come down to your sides, enjoying the slightly taller, wider sensation in your body. When people do this for about twenty seconds, you can clearly see the difference in them – they look taller, more confident, and more alert.

VOICE

We've all heard the phrase 'project your voice'. Ignore it. Light projects, but sound *resonates*. Attempting to 'project' your voice will cause effort and strain and reduce your vocal impact in the long run. It's more productive to focus on resonance. With your newly-alert body balanced on two feet, make a gentle, soft

'Hmmmm' sound, as if you were sinking into a lovely, warm bath or (in my case) eating plain, dark, organic chocolate. Try it now – 'Hmmmm'.

The 'H' is important, because it 'places' the sound at the front of your face, helping to avoid vocal tension. Following it with a gentle 'mmmm' helps to increase vocal resonance by gently vibrating the bones at the front of the face.

Do this gently and calmly, so that you avoid increasing tension.

Next, try saying a couple of words out loud that have lots of 'M's in them. This will help warm up your mouth and jaw at the same time as developing resonance – try words like 'marmalade' and 'mademoiselle'. I use the following phrase, partly because it makes me smile and partly because it encourages vocal resonance: 'Remember the money'. Try really exaggerating the 'M' and 'N' sounds, so that it sounds like 'Remmmmemmmber the mmmmonnnney'!

Now, try saying a sentence that forces you to think a bit. This is to ensure that your brain and voice are both working well and are ready to present. I don't recommend 'tongue twisters', since they can decrease your confidence if you get them wrong. I use the following sentence: 'When you write copy, you have the right to copyright the copy you write.' It's not a tongue-twister, but you do have to be awake and alert to say it.

Lastly, take the first line of your presentation and say it out loud. It doesn't matter if it's not the most interesting sentence, it could be as simple as 'Good morning everyone, thanks for coming to see my presentation today'. The point of doing this is to make sure that you're ready to present your message and yourself – not just intellectually, but physically too. Your body, mind, and voice are ready to go.

The above warm-up takes less than a minute and is easy to do. I've designed it to follow a careful sequence and to strike the perfect balance between being easy to do (so easy that there's no excuse for not doing it!) and being effective.

When you first come across the idea of a warm-up, it can seem like a strange idea. Many people treat the warm-up as a luxury extra, to be performed if and when they have time. Don't do this. Don't let the fact that this warm-up is simple deceive you. It works and will help you be a more compelling and confident presenter. Do it daily, and you'll notice a change in your 'presence'.

If you're really interested in improving your voice to a professional level, then the best route is to seek out a professional voice coach in combination with an Alexander Technique teacher and work with them for at least three months.

SIGNPOST

Practise the one-minute warm-up daily. In your next presentation, make sure that you've got a few minutes alone before your presentation starts so that you can warm up. Always say the first line of your presentation out loud a couple of times before you present.

Rehearsal, practice, and the important difference

I'm not a very good pianist, but I love having lessons. In one lesson, I was particularly nervous as I'd been working on a difficult piece. I played the piece. I fumbled, played wrong notes, and my timing was a bit rocky, to put it mildly. There was a pause. My teacher said, 'Ok, play it again'. I did. It was a little better.

My piano teacher said the phrase that performers all over the world hear every day – 'Once more, from the top.' I did. It was quite good. Fewer wrong notes, my timing was better, and I even began to enjoy playing the piece.

You've probably already realised that this story is about rehearsal and practice.

There's something important in this story, though, that is easy to miss. My teacher didn't give me any instructions or guidance. He just made me play the piece three times, and by the third attempt it had got better automatically.

Rehearsal and practice are the two most effective ways to make a presentation better, but most people avoid them. I think that there are three main reasons for this:

1. Rehearsal 'feels silly'. Almost every time I ask clients to rehearse, they go a little bit shy and say that they feel awkward.

2. Most people don't know the difference between practice and rehearsal. They think they're rehearsing when they're merely practising.

3. Most people underestimate rehearsal or think it's a luxury.

You *do* feel awkward when you rehearse, but that's the point of rehearsal – to get over that feeling *before* it matters. When you begin to rehearse, you start noticing how you sound to others, and you start spotting the gaps in your argument or the places where your presentation doesn't flow. You notice when the presentation is becoming boring or the data doesn't quite work. None of these things are enjoyable to notice, but it's crucial to spot them before the real presentation.

There is a difference between practice and rehearsal, and it's useful to know the difference. My piano story helps here. At home, I *practise* the piano. I play the notes at a speed that suits me, and I repeat them often enough to learn them. I can stop whenever I want. I can write reminders on the music. I am focused on the music, the keys of the piano, and what my hands are doing. At home, I sound ok.

The minute I start to play in front of my teacher, things change – I listen to myself more critically, my hands suddenly seem to gain a mind of their own, I get nervous, and my heart beats faster. Once I've started, I have to *keep going to the end*. I just don't play as well.

What's really happening is that when I practise I don't have the added stress of someone listening to me play, but that added stress is exactly what I need to improve. It's that stress that reveals where the weaknesses are in my playing. It's the fact that I have to keep going that makes rehearsing so different to practising.

For presentations, practising is simply making sure that the basics are there – that your slides are in the right order, that you know the flow of your presentation, that you have all the hand-outs and so on that you need, and that you know your hook and your punchline. When you practise, you can (and should) break the presentation into little sections and run through them.

Rehearsal is about, well, actually rehearsing. It means running through your presentation as close to the real-life situation as possible. It means that you start at the beginning and say the whole presentation, out loud, and go right through, without stopping, to the end.

Will you make mistakes? Yes. Will you want to change things? Yes. But that is the point of rehearsing. There are so many things that you can only find out by rehearsing – out loud – your presentation.

When I ask clients how much time they give to rehearsal, they often look a bit shifty and murmur something like, 'Well, Brian and I talked in the taxi about when he was going to do his bit and when I'm going to do mine.' This is *not* rehearsing. At best, this is setting up a running order.

Would you give a piano concert without rehearsing? Would you run a 10k race without training? Would you drive on a motorway on your first driving lesson? Of course not. Why should presentations be any different? When you present, you're doing something 'unnatural'. It takes a bit of work. You have to use your voice differently. You have to ensure that you know the running order well. You have to be clear about when to emphasise certain words and when to pause to let ideas sink in for a moment.

Being able to do these things is a skill. And it's as much a physical skill as a mental skill, which brings me to my golden rule of rehearsal: Don't rehearse in your head. 'Thinking through' what you're going to say is not enough. You have to rehearse!

HOW TO REHEARSE

Knowing how to do it is easy. Finding the discipline is harder. Put some time in your diary to rehearse, ideally a couple of days before most presentations and up to a week before an important one, to give yourself time to make changes.

Don't rehearse too early. Rehearsal should happen *after* the planning. Don't confuse rehearsal with 'figuring the presentation out'. You should rehearse once you've got most of the structure and once any slides are about 80% finished.

Make sure you're as close to 'real world' as possible. You need to rehearse with the same kind of equipment that you'll be using in the real presentation. If you're going to be delivering the presentation seated round a table with three other people, then try and book a similar room and rehearse 'as if' those people are there. If you're going to be presenting to a large room of people, with you on a raised platform, then try and get at least one rehearsal in a similar kind of space.

Don't stop! This is crucial, and it's the part most people get wrong in rehearsing. You need to go through your presentation exactly as if you were in front of a real audience. It's only by giving yourself this 'real-world' experience that you'll learn what works and what doesn't. Unless there's a serious technical problem, keep going. This builds confidence, and it also helps to develop the skill of thinking on your feet.

There will occasionally be problems and glitches in a presentation, so practising keeping going is a good skill to learn. More importantly, though, it's only when you rehearse your presentation without stopping that you get a genuine sense of whether the whole presentation is working or not, and whether the way that you're presenting it is correct.

Rehearse at least three times. This is non-negotiable – even for busy presenters. Make sure you've gone through your presentation, from start to finish, *at least* three times. In theatre, there's a rule that it takes an hour of rehearsal for every minute that you see on stage. And actors have lots of things that you don't – they have a playwright, a director, lighting designers, and costumes. You've got to write, direct, and perform the whole thing. If you've never rehearsed before, you'll be astonished at how quickly rehearsal can transform the quality of your presenting.

Record yourself. Record your first rehearsal and use it to get instant feedback. The pressure of the camera running will help you to rehearse better, too.

Time yourself. It's a hallmark of excellent presenters that they keep to time. Use your rehearsal time to learn how to do this.

Get an audience – even a fake one. I mean it. Where possible, for your third rehearsal ask a colleague or friend to be your audience. Their job is simple – to sit and watch you do your presentation and not let you stop. That's it. You'll find that the added pressure of even a single listener will really change how you deliver your presentation. If you really can't find someone to present to, then use something as a fake audience – a photograph of someone, a large cuddly toy, I even knew a client who used a mannequin! Yes, it's bonkers, but it's also effective – you'll find it much easier than you might expect to 'believe' in the audience.

SIGNPOST

· Rehearse your presentation at least three times.

· Record yourself.

· Use an audience for your last rehearsal.

How to sound confident

Kenny stood up to speak. He'd prepared well, he knew his argument, and he'd structured his thoughts carefully. But a couple of minutes into his presentation, his audience started getting restless. A couple of people were looking at their phones, and some were doodling. At the end of the presentation the questions were tough, and the tone was cynical. What caused this?

Kenny didn't *sound confident*. As well as having the

right message, sounding confident will help you get your message across to an audience. A lot of people, though, are confused about what 'sounding confident' really means or where true confidence comes from.

Real confidence in presenting does not come from 'attitude' or wishful thinking. It comes from three things: knowing your audience, knowing your message, and being well prepared. I often tell my clients to be 'slightly over-prepared'.

We've already covered almost everything you need to know to be confident with your message, but part of being well prepared is knowing that your voice will sound great. Doing the 'one-minute warm-up' regularly will help you develop a more confident-sounding voice that is likely to have the following characteristics:

It will be resonant. This is the single most important vocal quality. People with rich, resonant voices almost always sound more authoritative, credible, and confident.

It will be clear. Great speakers are always easy to understand. Their articulation is generally good, and they rehearse difficult words and phrases.

It will have variety. Great presenters are masters at controlling the variety of pitch and tone in their voices.

It will 'carry'. This is not the same as shouting. Great presenters often have a slightly 'metallic' edge to their voices, which means that the sound carries to the audience. This is just as important with an audience of three as an audience of three hundred.

Sometimes it stops. Great speakers are not afraid to pause and let a thought sink in. I often use this rule of thumb: 'Audiences can only start listening when you stop speaking'.

It will have some energy. Great presenters are so committed to their own message, and so connected to their desire to transmit that message, that there's always some energy in what they are saying. You don't need to fake this (in fact, you shouldn't), but you need to be sure that you're vocally invested in what you're saying.

It will be focused. Because the presenter is calm and confident, there will be very few 'filler' words. Great presenters tend not to use phrases such as 'Well, erm...' or 'Hopefully, I'm going to show you...' They have thought about what they're going to say, and they tell it to you without apology or hesitation.

Things to avoid if you want to sound confident:

Sounding 'breathy'. A lot of people become 'breathy' when they present. This reduces their impact, makes it harder to take them seriously, and sets up long-term vocal problems. Breathiness is usually caused by a nervous habit of taking quick, shallow breaths. The problem is that the breathier you get, the more nervous you feel, and the more nervous you feel, the more likely you are to become breathy!

Breathiness can usually be cured by learning how to relax the breathing. Ideally, set up a short daily routine to allow your breathing to be calm and free. It's important to have a 'base state' of calmness that you can return to when you're feeling stressed and nervous. One of the most effective methods for learning how to have calm, easy breathing is to study the Alexander Technique.

I always give myself a few moments before presenting to make sure that my breathing is calm and regular. I try not to speak to other people very much in the few minutes leading up to a presentation. This is partly because I want to gather my thoughts, but it's also because I want my breathing to be calm and natural.

Talking without pauses. This is one of the most common habits among unconfident presenters. They present with an 'I've got to get through this' mentality, which means they whiz through their presentations as fast as possible. Unfortunately, this has the effect of making the audience switch off and making the presenter look hurried and nervous. When rehearsing, make sure to practise some pauses. *The more important your point is, the more you need to pause around it*, so that an audience has time to understand it.

Being monotonous or staccato. Monotonous people sound as if the presentation is boring even to them! It's easy to avoid monotony: *rehearse*. If you know you have a habit of speaking in a monotone, then record yourself speaking and use the recording as your 'coach'. Speaking in a staccato style can make the presenter seem terrified, aggressive, or a mixture of both. Again, recording yourself is a great way to learn where you need to improve.

Talking too fast or too slow. I naturally speak fast – really fast! It almost causes me physical pain to slow down, but I have to. If I don't, my audience won't be able to understand what I'm saying. If they can't understand what I'm saying, then they will start to 'switch off' and I'll lose credibility with them. People who talk too fast often sound nervous or stressed.

Conversely, people who talk too slowly sound as if either they don't believe their own messages themselves or as if they are creating their presentation on the spur of the moment. They lose their audiences very quickly.

It's easy to solve these problems: record yourself during a real presentation. You only need to get about five minutes of recording to see what your vocal habits are. Then, practise the same part of your presentation, but deliberately emphasise the opposite of your habit – if you speak too fast, then deliberately speak… too… slow… ly. If you speak too slowly, speak really fast. Once you've done this a few times, you'll start to get a good sense of how to vary the pace and how to sound confidently in control of your material.

SIGNPOST

- Have you started practising the one-minute warm-up?
- Have you recorded yourself presenting and listed the two or three main improvements you need to make?
- Have you practised these improvements?
- Do you know how and when you'll pause in your next presentation?

The eyes have it

- Why is he staring at me? It's really weird.
- Why doesn't she look at us? Is she telling the truth?
- Hmmm. I'm not convinced.

Eye contact, or lack of it, can have a big effect on how your audience relates to your presentation. All of the comments above are things I've heard people say after watching presenters who had bad eye contact. Poor eye contact can lead an audience to doubt your message or find it hard to trust that you really believe what you're saying. It can indicate that you are nervous. It can lower your authority and distract your audience from your message.

It's not just the audience, though. Poor eye contact affects you too. Try staring at the floor as you say: 'I really believe in this proposal and I'm 100% confident that you'll benefit from it.' Can you feel how staring at the floor makes it harder for you to believe your own message?'

Eye contact is a powerful form of human communication, but it can go wrong when you're in the artificial environment of a business presentation. Bad eye contact can take several forms. I've named the most common types to avoid:

'Insects on the floor.' This describes a presenter who stares downwards all the time as if they are scared of crushing insects on the floor.

'I love the top of the back wall.' The presenter who stares above the heads of the audience – *for the whole presentation*.

'Where *did* you get those shoes?' The presenter who just seems to love the shoes of the front row and can't stop looking at them.

'Be my friend. Please.' The presenter who decides to only look at one or two people during the whole presentation and holds their eye contact for an uncomfortably long time.

'I love my notes.' The presenter who just looks at the notes the whole time.

'I can't remember my own name.' The presenter who needs to look at their slides during every moment of their presentation because they seem to have forgotten anything that's not written on a slide – even their own name.

'Have the police found me yet?' The presenter whose eyes are darting around all over the place, as if they're about to be found out.

I hope these descriptions made you smile – that's the point of them. If you can laugh about your eye contact faults, it's easier to correct them. I've had many coaching sessions where all I've needed to say is, 'Are those insects *still* there?' for my client to laugh and change their behaviour immediately.

When a presenter has good eye contact, the audience feels involved and engaged, but not stared at or intimidated. How can you do this?

Here again, the Rule of Three helps. Mentally divide your audience into three sections (either left, middle, and right, or front, middle, and back, depending on how they're seated) and make sure that each section receives an equal amount of eye contact from you. Spread your eye contact between the three sections of the audience, and spend two to four seconds with each section at a time.

Another useful technique, especially when there are more than about ten people in the audience, is to *look very slightly above people's eyes* – just at the level of the eyebrows. It sounds crazy, but it has the effect of making the audience feel like you're engaging them without making it feel awkward – to you or to them.

It's also helpful to *'sweep' the audience*. Although holding direct eye contact is uncomfortable for most people, 'sweeping' is easy and helps everyone feel included. As you're talking, occasionally look across the whole audience at direct eye level, as if you're sweeping the room with your eyes. This is a useful technique to combine with dividing the audience into three sections – you can 'sweep' from one section to another.

Watch for reactions. Good eye contact is not just a technique, it's also a tool for sensing how engaged your audience is with you. If you're genuinely interested in the audience's reactions you'll find it easier to have natural, genuine eye contact. You'll also pick up useful information about your audience. Are they held rapt by your amazing message, or are they daydreaming?

Prepare 'eye contact moments'. In most presentations, there will be moments when it's important to have the audience's full attention – often at the end of a thought, or when you're introducing a new topic or point. Unfortunately, many presenters choose exactly these moments to look down at their notes or at the slides. Decide where these moments should be and rehearse them. It takes a bit of courage to choose to hold eye contact at important moments, but you'll get used to it quickly.

What do I do with my hands?

'I often find that when I start presenting, especially standing up, I don't know what to do with my hands, and they seem to take on a life of their own.'

People say versions of this over and over again.

It's probably a familiar situation to any of you who've had to speak in front of a group. Apart from the dry mouth and pounding heart, as soon as you start speaking your hands decide to dance around entirely on their own. In an attempt to tame them, you grip a lectern, or shove them in your pockets, or cross your arms, but nothing seems to work. They fight back, and they *always* win!

There are two ways of solving this problem. One way seems to be popular with 'presentation skills trainers' and that is to give a list of rules, such as 'move your hands like this', or 'here are some power poses – use these'. However, in my experience this style of teaching doesn't work well, for all the reasons given in the section on nerves earlier in this chapter – it's not natural to stand up in front of a group. Your old lizard brain is trying to get you to run away from the stressful situation, and so you become muscularly tense.

Once you realise this, you see that getting a list of rules can't help you tame your hands because rules can't help you deal with the underlying condition. If your lizard brain is trying to get you to run away, and you're trying to use 'power gestures', you just create more tension and the problem gets worse. It's a bit like taking an aspirin for a tooth infection.

Here's what you can do:

- **Make sure you're prepared and practised.** The more prepared you are, the less your brain tries to make you run away.

- **Do the one-minute warm-up.** The more often you do it, the more relaxed and confident you'll feel.

- **A prop often helps.** Many people feel more secure presenting when they have a clicker, a bottle of water, a microphone, or even just a piece of paper. (Steve Jobs, the master of presenting, usually had something in his hands for most of his presentations).

- **Plan a few natural gestures** that support your message (see below).

But here's the real secret:

- **Connect to your message.** Your hands don't behave strangely when you're chatting to your friends or telling someone how to get to the train station. Why not? Because you know what your message is, and you want the person to understand it. Almost always, hands 'misbehave' because our awareness is on ourselves rather than the audience and the message.

So ask yourself again, 'What do I want my audience to do, or to know, or to feel as a result of my presentation?' When you're really clear about that message, and you really want your audience to get it, most of your tension problems will fade away.

GESTURES

- There are three main points I'd like to cover today…
- When we began we were tiny – a really tiny business. And we stayed that way for a long time. Recently, we've grown. We've grown a lot.
- This challenge is serious. It's not a 'difficulty', it's an obstacle preventing us from getting off the starting block.

Some phrases just *demand* physical gestures, don't they? I'm not recommending being fake, just using clear natural gestures that support your message. As always, make sure that you're clear about your message and that you're committed to it. If you don't believe what you're saying, no amount of gestures will make you appear more credible or believable.

Once you're certain of what you're saying, decide on a few moments when you'd like to emphasise what you're saying with a gesture and, as Hamlet said, 'Suit the action to the word, the word to the action.'

Getting gestures right isn't difficult. Getting them right in real time in front of an audience when you haven't rehearsed is what's difficult. Most gestures are obvious. If you're talking about a company growing, you can indicate that by raising a hand. If the company's shrinking, bring your hands together. If you're talking about an 'obstacle preventing us getting us off the starting block', then you can indicate the block with a fist or by bringing your hands together. What's not obvious is that you should prepare for these moments. Try a few out as you practise, and then use the ones you like in your rehearsal. Stick to gestures that feel natural but also emphasise your point.

Gestures are like slides – they should *support* your message, not detract from it.

There's an added benefit to learning a few gestures. Every actor will tell you that gestures and movement help them learn their lines, and it's the same for you as a presenter. If you practise some gestures, especially during important parts of your message, you get mental 'hooks' that help you to remember the structure of your presentation without having to look at slides every three seconds.

I make sure that I've got one meaningful gesture for each of the important parts of my presentation – the hook, each of the three main points, and my punchline. They help me to pace my presentation, to reinforce important points, and to remember what I'm supposed to be saying.

If you're unsure about any of the gestures that you're thinking of using, record yourself on your phone's camera and choose the ones that look best and feel natural.

SIGNPOST

Make sure that you:

- Have practised your presentation with relaxed arms and hands.

- Are ready with some natural, but practised, gestures for key moments.

- Know how to do a one-minute warm-up.

Move the body

There's one final type of gesture worth practising – moving your entire body. This is particularly relevant if you're presenting on a stage in front of a large audience, but it's also useful even sitting in a small space.

It might not sound like a 'gesture', but how you move your entire body in space sends a message to the audience. Imagine, for example, a presenter who said, 'I'd now like to take questions' but moved away from the audience as they were saying that. Or imagine a presenter who said, 'My most important point is this' but started to walk across the stage for no apparent reason. It would look odd, and it would undermine the message. Audiences won't consciously know that your 'choreography' isn't congruent with your message, but they will sense it. They'll believe you less and possibly switch off entirely.

In theatre, there are terms for moving in different parts of the performing space, and you can use these to your advantage in your own presenting. 'Upstage' means the area farthest from the audience. 'Downstage' is closest to the audience. 'Left' and 'right' are from the presenter's perspective.

Have a look at the following Busy Person's crib sheet for the performing space:

UPSTAGE

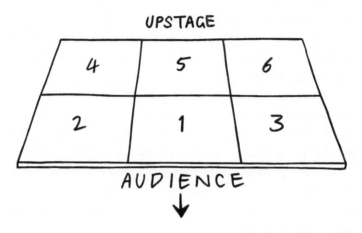

AUDIENCE
↓

I've divided the performing area into six sections. Imagine that you're standing in Square 1. This is centre stage – the 'diva spot' (downstage centre). Ideally, aim to be here for the beginning, ending, and any important messages in your presentation. This is the spot to be in when you say, 'There's one crucial lesson we all need to take from the data…' If you can't use this space (because of a projector beam), then try to get as close to it as possible. I've even asked for projectors to be moved so that I can use this space.

Squares 2 and 3 are downstage left and right. These spaces are excellent for taking questions and for moments when you want to be connected with the audience but don't necessarily have a major point to make. These are the spaces to move into when you say things like: 'I'm sure you have lots of questions, and I'm happy to take those now…' and 'So let's think about how this data is useful for us…'

Avoid Square 5. It's amazing how many presenters retreat to this space (upstage centre), but if there's a screen with slides then you don't want to be in front of it. And even if there's no screen, you just look scared and you lose impact if you spend any time in this space. Don't be a wall-hugger.

Square 4 (upstage right) is useful when you have made your main point and want to expand on it a little. It's a great space to move into when you've just made the audience think a bit and want to relax the tone. Key phrases here include: 'That's a lot of information, let me boil it down to a simple idea…' This is also the ideal space if you're asking people to look at something on a slide.

Square 6 (upstage left) is similar to Square 4, but with one addition. This space is perfect for bringing on props, surprises, and anything new. If you're going to show a product to the audience or introduce something new, like a brochure or new logo design, then bring it on from Square 6. Don't ask me why this works, it just does. I'm sure one day somebody will do a PhD in why audiences react in certain ways to certain areas of the stage, but until then just try it out.

Plan a few moments when you are going to move for a reason. For example, if you've been giving some detailed information from Square 4, and you now want the full attention of the audience, then plan to move from Square 4 to Square 1 as you say something like: 'There's one crucial thing that this strategy means for us...' By the time you say the word 'us', aim to be bang in the centre of the stage – you'll be amazed at how it gathers the attention of the audience.

Planning some 'choreography' for your presentation is easy to do, and you'll instinctively feel when you've got it right and wrong. It's one of the quickest ways to have the audience hanging on your every word.

Notes and props

NOTES

'Am I allowed to use notes?' I hear this question all the time. You've probably thought it yourself. The Busy Person's answer is yes.

Presenting is not a memory test or a mental assault course. It's about one thing and one thing only: affecting people with your message. Anything that helps you to do that is welcome – including notes.

Practice and rehearsal are the best times to work out what kind of notes you might need. The better you know your audience, your goal, and your material, the fewer notes you'll need. I present a lot and usually have one word or one picture on a slide to remind me of where I am in a presentation. That's enough for some people, but most would like a little more security.

Blank index cards work very well. Get the kind that you can put a small bit of string through in the top corner – it holds them together if you drop the cards! Also, number the cards just in case you get lost.

When you practise, try just writing one key word per card so that you're covering the main thoughts. For example, card 1 might have your goal on it, card 2 the hook, and so on.

As you practise, you might discover that you need two or three extra words on some of the index cards, just to keep the flow going, so feel free to write them in. Get a marker pen for the big keyword, and then a thick felt-tip for the secondary words. Make it easy for yourself to see the main point, even under the stress of live presenting.

Then, rehearse with the cards. You'll soon find out whether there's enough information on them to keep you going. You might find out that you don't need them nearly as much as you thought you did!

Avoid writing out any kind of word-for-word script. A presentation is not a speech, and it's rare that a business audience expects performer-level eloquence. It's easy to lose your way in a script, and moments of rustling through sheets of A4 paper trying to find where you are can quickly lower your credibility. It's better to stick to minimal notes.

If you're confident without notes but need a little more security than just your slides, then try something that I do: add a small word, in a very faint font on the bottom corner of each slide, reminding you of what's on the *next* slide. Your audience will never notice it, but you'll know it's there if you need it.

Lastly, make two copies of your notes. One day, you'll be very glad that you did!

PROPS

'Props' is the theatre term for any physical object used on stage.

I'm a big fan of props. They can often add life to a presentation, and sometimes humour. When Steve Jobs launched the MacBook Air, he dramatically pulled it out of an envelope. It was a brilliant use of a prop to make a point more powerfully than words could.

However, props are like the girl with the curl – when they're used well, they are very, very good, and when they're used badly, they're horrid.

Here are the ground rules:

Props are exactly like slides – they must *support* your message, not detract from it. It's agonising to watch someone who's using a prop to disguise the fact that they haven't prepared well enough. I once saw a presentation where the presenter kept mentioning that the audience had to 'throw your hat in the ring'. As you've guessed, he wore a hat, and every time he used the phrase he threw his hat onto the floor. It was cute the first time he did it, by the fourth time it was ridiculous.

Anything physical can be a prop. Hand-outs, feedback forms, surveys, and brochures all qualify, as do products and models.

If you're going to use a prop, it's essential to practise. Where are you going to get the prop from? Where will you return it to? Can the audience see it clearly? Does it have any buttons, alarms, fiddly bits, or anything else that could go wrong in a live event? If so, practise dealing with it. I once worked with a tech client who had to use gaffer tape at the last minute to stop a button being pressed accidentally during a presentation!

Keep your props a surprise if you can. There's something dramatic about taking a prop out of a box, or lifting off a cloth, or going offstage to get it. Audiences like pleasant surprises, and bringing in a surprise prop can make your presentation more varied and interesting.

Another way to use a prop is to build some suspense around the 'reveal'. Many great presenters use this technique. For example, early in your presentation you can hold up a hand-out and mention the important information it contains and that you'll give it out at the end. About two thirds of the way through your presentation, you can hold it up again and mention another important piece of information in the hand-out and remind the audience that you'll leave it with them at the end. Using the prop intrigues your audience, and you can guarantee they'll all want the hand-out.

SIGNPOST

Notes:

- Have you prepared your notes?
- Have you written your keywords and secondary words clearly?
- Have you rehearsed with your notes?
- Have you made a spare copy of your notes?
- Have you added a word to each slide to remind you of what's coming next?

> Props:
>
> · Have you decided which props are good to use in a live presentation?
>
> · Have you decided how you will use each prop during the presentation?
>
> · Have you practised using/displaying each prop?
>
> · Do you have a 'Plan B' if a prop fails or breaks?
>
> · Can you find a way to make the 'reveal' of each prop interesting?

You're joking!

If you're naturally funny, and you know you are, you can skip this chapter. The rest of you, read on. But seriously…

I was working with the managing partner of a global accountancy firm, and I asked him to show me his presentation. It quickly became clear that he was uncomfortable with his delivery. He looked and sounded awkward, and there was a lack of energy and commitment in his presenting style.

We did some work to improve his message, and the presentation was a bit better, but there was still something not quite right. I couldn't put my finger on it. I asked him how he felt about the presentation, and he replied: 'I feel fine, except I'm not comfortable with being funny. I don't think I'm very good at it.'

'Why do you have to be funny?' I asked. 'Just get the message across.'

He looked a bit shocked and said, 'But I thought presenters were supposed to be funny?'

'It's not the law!' I replied.

A look of relief spread across his face. 'Well, that's true, isn't it? Why have I been beating myself up about it?'

'Well, let's try it again. Be friendly, but don't force being funny,' I encouraged.

His presentation was more natural and engaging and, strangely, it was genuinely amusing in parts because he relaxed and let his own style come through. I'm telling you this story because many people think that they have to 'be funny' in their presenting, but it's not true. Don't give yourself this burden.

Some people are naturally funny, and audiences just warm to them. But it's a rare gift. Most of us don't have that talent. The problem is that if you give yourself the burden of trying to 'be funny', then the temptation can be to rely on 'jokes' – often awful puns and one-liners only slightly better than those from a Christmas cracker.

There are few rules in this book. But here's one: Avoid jokes.

Here's the next: Use humour often.

These two rules do not contradict each other. Jokes and humour are very different in their effects on an audience.

Any presentation will benefit from humour. Audiences love to smile and laugh. It helps them to relax and engage with the presenter. Anyone who is in a good mood is likely to agree with the presenter more and remember their message. A self-deprecating comment, a shared reference, a topical story, a bit of fun at the expense of some jargon or industry nonsense – all of these things can be delightful in a presentation, and I encourage my clients to use them as often as they can. You don't need to be naturally funny to use humour; audiences appreciate the attempt more than the skill with which it's delivered.

Jokes, however, are different. It's hard to get a joke right and all too easy to get one wrong. To get a joke a right, you need expert timing, a good instinct for the taste of your audience, a flawless delivery, and the guarantee that nobody will accidentally take offense. Don't give yourself the stress of telling jokes. Focus on humour instead.

It's a strange fact, but very few comedians tell jokes. Let that sink in for a moment. What they usually do is tell stories with surprising or funny endings, or they present familiar things back to us in surprising ways, and that is what makes them funny.

In his wonderful book *Laughter: A Scientific Investigation*, the American scientist Robert Provine presents the first scientific study of why humans laugh, and what he says is directly relevant to presenters:[5] 'Most laughter is not in response to jokes.'

In Provine's studies, he claims that only 10–20% of 'laughter episodes' are caused by anything resembling a joke. Laughter is actually a function of signalling to the group that you're 'part of the crowd'. So shared comments, and things that the audience all understand

---

5. Provine, R (2000) *Laughter: A Scientific Investigation*, London, Penguin.

are humorous, work well in helping an audience to smile, laugh, and bond together. That probably explains why self-deprecating humour almost always works well.[6]

Allow yourself to relax, and just share stories, comments, and jargon that the audience will find amusing. Don't try to 'be funny', just get your message across, do it with a smile, and allow the audience to enjoy the presentation with you.

The funny thing is – the less effort you make, the funnier people will think you are.

SIGNPOST

Check your presentation for 'jokes' – take them out unless you're 100% confident about them. Are there opportunities for humour? Try to use humour every ten minutes or so. Think of making audiences smile in recognition, rather than trying for laughter.

Any questions?

I deliberately provoke questions during my presentations. I try and stimulate the audience's thinking, but I often leave out certain details just to inspire some questions. I do this because questions can be the most interesting part of a presentation. It's where you see what a presenter is really made of and how deep their

---

6. Provine, R, 'Laughter', *American Scientist*, 84, 1/1996: 38–47.

knowledge is. For many audiences, questions can be the most important part of a presentation.

Many people, though, either try to avoid questions or handle them badly – often by leaving just a few minutes at the end of the presentation, rushing through the answers, and then finishing on the most difficult question or a badly-worded answer.

Preparation is the best way to become good at handling questions. There are usually four types of questions asked during presentations:

1. Questions that you're ready for and confident with.
2. Questions that you're ready for but would rather not hear.
3. Questions that are a surprise but that you're confident and comfortable with.
4. Questions that are a surprise and that you wish you hadn't been asked!

The good news is that there's a Busy Person's way to prepare in advance for all of these types of questions:

Prepare for the obvious questions. You should know your material and your audience well enough that you can predict obvious questions. Are people going to ask you about budgets, deadlines, resources, and so on? Practise responding to these questions *out loud* during your rehearsal.

Set the ground rules. Be ready to let people know near the start of your presentation whether or not you're happy to take questions during the presentation, and stick to the rule (see below for how to deal with interruptions). Take a moment to decide on the wording that you'll use. For example, 'I'd like to keep this informal, so do ask questions as we go' if that's your style, or 'There will be plenty of time at the end of the presentation to ask questions, and I'll be happy to answer them then.' Clarity over when to ask questions is crucial on a conference call or web-based presentation.

Be clear about the structure of your presentation, as this will help you deal with interruptions. If you always know what your next main point is, you don't get thrown by unexpected questions.

Prepare some easy questions for yourself that the audience probably needs answers to. It's common for presentations to have an awkward pause when the presenter says: 'So, any questions?' If you prepare a few easy questions for yourself, you can fill this pause easily by saying: 'Well, several of you are probably wondering...'

You can also use these 'easy' questions if you are asked a question that is too complex to answer in your allowed time. You might say, 'That's a difficult question to answer in the time we've got; can I follow up with you after? But it reminds me of a similar question...', and replace the complex question with your similar, but easier and simpler, question.

Lastly, you can use your pre-prepared easy questions if the questions you do receive are a bit boring or strange or feel flat. When you know the questions are coming to an end, just finish with one of your own, so that the final impression of your question answering is a positive one.

Practise saying out loud, 'I don't know the answer to that. I'll find out and get back to you.' Embrace honesty. Nobody can be expected to know the answer to every question, and sometimes 'I don't know' is the best answer to a question.

HANDLING INTERRUPTIONS

'What do I do if people interrupt my presentation with impossible questions and try to trip me up?'

Remember, it's not 'your' presentation. It belongs to the audience too. It's rare that someone will ask you a question to trip you up deliberately. They nearly always ask 'impossible' questions for one of three reasons: they really do want the answer, they want to look good in front of the other audience members, or they're just not very good at phrasing a question.

If you've laid the ground rules as above, you'll already be on safe ground for most questions, but the following 'RAB' technique will get you out of almost any difficult question.

RAB: **R**epeat – **A**nswer – **B**ridge

Repeat the question out loud – every time. I do this with every single question I get. I do it for three reasons: so that everyone hears it, to make sure that I've listened to the question properly, and to give myself time to think of an answer!

Answer the question. This is the obvious middle bit. Give a brief answer, sticking only to the main point of the question. If you think that there were several points in the question, or that the point is vague, *clarify* the main point when you repeat the question: 'So, as I understood it, the main point of your question is that you're worried we won't have the resources to guarantee finishing this project within four months, is that right?'

Bridge to your next or main point. This is the 'secret sauce' that will help you appear to be a world-class presenter. Don't stop with just your answer. Check with the questioner that they're happy with what you've said (I often say things like, 'As a brief response, does that answer your question for now?'), and then bridge back to your main point.

There are two type of 'bridging' – bridging *up* and bridging *down*. Bridging up means that you take the topic *up* to the main point of your presentation. Bridging down is the opposite – you take a grand and vague question and bring it *down* to the main point of your presentation. For example:

Bridging up: 'So, if we take this project on, we can be confident that we'll have the resources to finish it – does that answer your question?' (Questioner nods 'yes'.) 'But the resources aren't the most important thing. The most important thing – (bridging up) – is what this project says about our company and its values over the next few years.'

Bridging down: 'Yes, I think you're right that we're all worried about the retention of long-term clients, and outside of this presentation I can send you some strategies that we're currently working on to help with that. Would that be ok?' (Questioner nods 'yes'.)... It's important, though, not to lose sight of specifics – (bridging down) – because on a day-to-day level it's our personal interactions with clients, and the quality of our work, that matters. It's about how our clients react to our company every day.'

Bridging is an expert technique that is easy to learn and will help you go almost seamlessly from any question back to your main point.

SIGNPOST

· Are you prepared for obvious questions?

· Are you clear on your structure, so you can deal with interruptions?

· Have you prepared some 'just in case' questions of your own?

· Have you practised RAB?

· Have you practised bridging up and down?

Deadly distractions

There are many advantages to arriving early for your presentation, and one of the biggest is being able to remove distractions.

Recently, I arrived to give a presentation to forty people and realised, to my horror, that the organisers had set the audience chairs facing a glass wall. This meant that my audience would have spent my entire presentation staring at, and being stared at by, all the people working on the other side of the wall! I had to gently put my foot down and move the chairs to face another direction. I was only able to do this because I'd arrived early.

Arrive early and look at the presenting space from the audience's point of view. If you can, try and sit in a couple of the seats that the audience will use and look at the space you'll be presenting in. This will be useful regardless of whether you're presenting on a large stage or sitting in a small meeting room. Ask yourself, 'If I were the audience, would I find anything distracting or annoying from where I'm sitting?'

In particular, look for moving distractions – people through glass walls(!), bits of paper blowing on a corkboard, creaky floorboards, air-conditioning above your head, a door moving in the breeze, a projector screen swaying squeakily (I've suffered from all of these).

Look also for bright colours, text, posters, and images behind you. Check that any lighting is falling on to you, rather than falling from behind you towards the audience. Look out for pillars that block anyone's view and for any tables or chairs placed at strange angles. If possible, try to present at the opposite end of the room to any doors. This means that if people arrive late or need to leave early it's less distracting for everyone.

This is also a good time to check that you have everything you need for your presentation. Make sure your notes are ready and that you have a glass of water nearby (I always prefer a plastic bottle with a cap, as it reduces the chance of knocking it over disastrously).

Sometimes, despite all your efforts, distractions happen that you can't prevent, such as an important phone call, an audience member falling ill, or someone spilling something. The best way to deal with these is to acknowledge them, remember where you are in the structure of your presentation, and then continue as soon as you're able.

Don't ignore distractions. The more you try and ignore them, the more obvious they are to the audience. As soon as you acknowledge them, the audience can relax and it's easier for you to continue.

CHAPTER FOUR

The Busy Person's Guide To Slides

Do without

Once upon a time there were no slides, and yet somehow people still managed to get their messages across. Socrates, Napoleon, Lincoln, and Churchill, as well as all the great religious leaders, managed to engage and inspire their audiences without slides. As far as I know, no one ever heard Jesus or the Buddha say, 'I'll tell you the parable as soon as I've hooked up this projector.'

The ultimate Busy Person's approach to slides is to do without them completely. This isn't as scary as it might sound. When you're preparing your presentation, I strongly recommend that you go through the entire message structure – goal, hook, three main points, questions, and punchline – *before* you start thinking about whether or not to use slides.

You have to know your message before you can

choose the medium. Only when you've finished creating your message, and have identified who your audience is, can you really answer the question, 'Do I need any slides?' You might be surprised to see how often the answer is, 'No, I don't. The presentation is fine as it is.'

Sometimes you'll find that you do need slides and other visual aids, but waiting until you've set the structure before deciding brings many benefits:

- You will be much clearer about your message and how you're going to deliver it.

- Your delivery will be more natural and confident, since you'll know your message much better.

- You will be technology-proof, and it saves time and stress. No fiddling about with software, no scrabbling around on the floor trying to plug in a stray cable. No panic because someone forgot the USB stick. After all, if you're not using slides (or at least not reliant on them) there's not too much else that can go wrong with technology.

- You will engage your audience more. Your body language and eye contact will be more natural. Audiences can easily sense whether someone really knows and cares about their presentation or whether they're just reading from slides.

- You will probably enjoy the experience more than you expect. I have many clients who've said variations of: 'I was terrified of presenting without slides, but actually I enjoyed it. It felt more like a conversation and was much less formal.'

- You'll be more memorable. People who present without slides stand out almost automatically, because no one else does it. I have a client who had decided that they needed some slides for a client presentation. When they arrived at the client offices and were setting up, they realised that the PowerPoint file had become corrupted. They had to make a choice: spend the time trying to repair the slides, or just do without. They did without and used the time to remind themselves of their goal and their main message. The potential client was so impressed at their natural, intelligent approach that the 'presentation' quickly turned into a consultation, and my client walked away being asked to pitch for a much bigger project than they'd expected – and they eventually won it.

Walking into a room with just your ideas and a few notes can be very liberating – for you and the audience.

> **SIGNPOST**
>
> Are you clear about your presentation message, structure, and intended audience? If you're not, you're not ready to think about slides yet!

Use an expert

Once you've got your message structure right, in many cases you will decide that you do need to use slides. If you've worked through the structure, however, you'll nearly always find that you need fewer slides than you think, and you'll be clearer and more precise about the function of each slide.

When you *really* need slides, the Busy Person's way is to use an expert to create them. In larger firms, you'll have in-house departments or regular freelancers. For everyone else, there are many online services where you can find great designers at affordable rates. I had an entire slide deck designed recently for the price of three coffees, and the slides were much better than the coffee.

HOW TO CHOOSE A DESIGNER

The best way to choose an online designer is by looking at previous examples of their work (ideally alongside the brief they were given, so that you can judge their ability to deliver what's asked) as well as testimonials from certified employers. Most online systems have five-star ratings, but look also at the number of jobs they've delivered on. I'd rather use someone rated at four stars with 900 completed jobs than someone rated at five stars with three completed jobs.

If you're going to use an expert it's important to give them a clear brief, but try to avoid being too restrictive. This is true for both in-house experts and freelancers.

Let the designer know:

- Who your audience is.
- What your main goal is.

- The 'structure' of your presentation – give them clarity over the flow of your message.
- How you want the audience to 'feel' during the presentation.
- Give them a feel for how you want it to look – I mock up some rough examples.
- Send them examples of any presentation slides and images you like.
- Send them any useful corporate colours and logos.

Don't:

- Micro-manage.
- Send them finished slides to 'pretty up' (you'll usually get a better result if you let them create their own ideas from rough drafts).
- Be too restrictive on the look – give them some ideas but also space to create. You'll be pleasantly surprised at the result.
- Settle for a first draft. Be ready to work on adjustments.

When you get the slides, don't judge them just on aesthetic appeal. Load them up and have a quick practice run, looking at them from an audience's point of view.

Do ask:

- Do the slides *support* my message?
- Are they simple? Will an audience 'get' them quickly without having to do any mental work?

- Are they consistent? (Do any images look weirdly larger than others? Do the fonts change too much, etc.)

- Are there any distractions on the slides?

- Are there enough changes to keep the audience's interest? (This doesn't contradict the previous two points – you want enough change to keep people interested, but nothing jarring, clumsy, or ugly.)

- Are there any pointless slides? (Has the designer added anything like a 'Thank you' slide, which might be superfluous?)

- Is there a theme, either in fonts, in design, or in images?

- Is everything clear *to me*? I have seen too many presenters who've forgotten what a particular slide is about and had to refer to their notes. Instead, make the slide more obvious to you at first glance.

- Do I feel good presenting with them?

- Lastly, it can be useful to ask the designer to make you a 'master slide'. You may find that you need to make a few extra slides at the last minute, and having the template will save you a lot of time!

If you're going to give the same presentation a lot, in different places, it can be worthwhile asking for the slides in PowerPoint, Keynote (for Mac), and as PDFs. This will mean that you're ready to present in almost any environment.

SIGNPOST

Good freelancer sites are:

· www.graphicriver.net (here you can buy a template you like and ask the designer to customise it for you).

· www.upwork.com and www.fiverr.com (every type of freelancer you'll ever need).

· www.peopleperhour.com (similar to Upwork, with a clear rating and review system).

Do it yourself

The sometimes unavoidable option is to do the slides yourself.

A mistake almost everyone makes with their own slides is to fire up PowerPoint and think: 'What information do I need to put on the slide *for me* as the presenter?'

There are several reasons to avoid this:

- You'll nearly always end up with far too many slides.

- The slides will often act as a 'script' for you and be full of text.

- You'll start forgetting about your goal and just think about transmitting information.

- You'll end up spending lots of time formatting the slides, instead of getting your message right and rehearsing.

Instead, here's a quick way to keep yourself on track if you DIY your slides – ask yourself the question: 'What does the audience need to see to understand my message?' In fact, don't just ask yourself – write it down on a post-it note and stick it next to your computer as you're creating the slides.

Keeping this question at the front of your mind while creating your slides has many benefits:

- You'll have fewer slides.

- You'll be more focused on your message and goal.

- Your audience will enjoy your presentation more as the slides will be aimed at them rather than a support for you.

- Your audience will be more likely to act on your ideas because they'll understand them more clearly.

STYLE

If you work for a company that already has a standard look to the slides, then it's fairly easy to just copy the template. If you don't have that resource, then a Busy Person's way to get going is to look at some slides you like (you can find thousands of examples online) and use those as inspiration. Obviously, don't copy anyone else's work or copyrighted material, but you can learn a lot about spacing, design, and colours just by looking at other people's slides.

I'm not a designer, so I'll always try to use an expert if I need slides. However, when I have to make my own slides, these guidelines have helped me a lot:

Keep the slides simple. You can always fill in detail with spoken words and hand-outs. Your slides should never be the star of the show, so resist the temptation to complicate them.

Think visually, not in terms of content. Slides are for visuals. Content is for brochures, hand-outs, and books.

Stick to the Rule of Three – have no more than three pieces of information on any one slide or at any one moment.

Have a consistent 'feel'. Make sure that logos are all the same colour, that images are all the same size, and that all fonts are consistent. Stick to a colour palette of just a few colours. I don't recommend using pre-loaded templates (especially in PowerPoint) as they can be too restrictive. I tend to make a couple of 'master slides' and then just duplicate those each time I need a new slide so that they all look consistent.

Have a few surprises. While consistency is important, you don't want all of your slides to look identical. Have a few visual surprises to keep your audience's interest. For example, if I use ten slides, I'll aim for seven of them to be large images and three to be just text – perhaps with one or two large words on a blank background.

Signal the changes. If you're moving from one part of a presentation to another – for example, from 'Where we are' to 'Where we need to be' – think of using an image, colour change, or anything that will help the audience understand that the presentation is moving on to something new.

Tell a visual story. If your presentation has a clear 'journey' or 'story', your slides can mirror that. For example, a client of mine was using the metaphor of unwrapping a present to explain to his audience that there were many unknowns to the future of their company but that they were slowly uncovering something important.

On his first slide, he had a picture of a beautifully-wrapped present. On subsequent slides, below the data, he had a smaller image of the present. On each slide, the present was a little more unwrapped – first the ribbon, then bits of paper, and so on until the end of the presentation. His last slide showed a simple picture of a fully unwrapped present with a giant question mark inside. It was a delightful way to tell a visual story that supported his presentation.

Avoid bullet points. There's rarely a need for them in any presentation these days – it's not 1996. The reason that bullet points were invented was to make text clearer, but you don't need that in a presentation. It's clearer to devote a slide to each point rather than listing all of them on a single slide. Either something's worth presenting, or it's not. If it is, then give it its own slide.

Make things easy for yourself. Remember my advice in the section on notes in Chapter Three: to help me remember what's coming next, I write a word on each slide that reminds me of the next one. I write the word in very small, faint text at the bottom right corner of each slide. I know it's there, so it's easy for me to see, but the audience aren't looking for it, so it's invisible to them.

TITLES

Titles are a terrific Busy Person's way to instantly improve a slide deck. I spend a lot of my preparation time thinking about the titles of my presentations and slides.

A good title will fulfil at least one of the following qualities:

- Be intriguing;
- Be humorous;
- Be provocative;
- Help the audience focus;
- Make you look good in advance;
- Build anticipation;
- Be clear but not boring.

For example, a client of mine changed their presentation name from 'Marketing Update Q4' to: 'Three months to fix things'.

Another client was going to present 'Social Media Strategy for New Client Acquisition'. He changed it to: 'They're on Instagram, why aren't we?'

And this book could have been called *A Guide to Business Presentations*. But you (probably) wouldn't have bought that one. You did buy this one, though!

Slides or hand-outs?

Many people get confused about the difference between slides and hand-outs. There seems to be an unwritten rule that audiences should be sent the slides from a presentation, and so the slides should also be written as stand-alone hand-outs, full of all the information that the audience needs outside of your presentation.

But come back to the golden rule of presenting: A presentation is not about information, it's about how you affect your audience with that information.

Your slides should be a support for your presenting, not a substitute for it. Your hand-outs should cover the details that you don't have time for in your presentation. This means that usually it's a good idea to make your hand-outs separate from the slides.

The hand-outs should deepen your message and add more details, facts, and figures to back up the message in your presentation. Your presentation should be focused on getting emotional commitment for your goal. Your hand-outs can do all the heavy lifting in terms of content and data. Hand-outs should remind people of the main goal and key points of your presentation and give all the essential extra details that people need to make a decision or continue the conversation.

HOW TO PREPARE HAND-OUTS

When you're confident of the structure of your presentation, and you know which slides you're going to use, then print them out – one slide per page. On the back of each slide, make notes to yourself about the extra things your audience might need to know *after* your presentation that you won't have time for during the presentation.

Ask yourself:

- What questions will the audience have at this point?
- What extra data do I need to reinforce the point I'm making at this moment?
- Are there any other case studies, testimonials, or anecdotes that would make this part of the presentation more convincing?
- Is there anything I need to add here to increase trust and confidence in my presentation?
- Is there any extra reading or resources that I can point the audience to?
- Are there any doubts that people might have at the end of the presentation that I can address in the hand-outs?

WHEN TO HAND OUT THE HAND-OUTS

I recommend leaving hand-outs until the end, or very near the end, of your presentation. When you're presenting you need the audience's attention, and it's difficult to get that if they're also looking at hand-outs. However, it's often a good idea to mention the hand-outs earlier, and even show them to the audience without letting them have them straightaway. This gives you two benefits: you keep the audience's attention and, because they've been made to wait for the hand-outs, they usually take them more seriously.

A good presenter will often say something like, 'All the details are contained in this hand-out... [holds it up – it looks shiny and lovely, and there's a hint of an exciting graphic]... which I'll hand out at the end of the presentation' (puts the hand-out down; the audience leans eagerly towards it). You get the idea.

Hand-outs can also be used for the things that might feel awkward during the presentation, such as lengthy client testimonials, longer company biographies, long-term project processes, and calls-to-action.

If people are likely to use your hand-outs with others (for example, if you're pitching for something and they're going to show your hand-outs internally), then the same rules apply as to slides: keep things simple, make sure your main messages are obvious, and 'Don't bury your headline' – make sure the key information is big, bold, and at the front, and keep all the technical, detailed information lower down the page or at the end. Make it easy for anyone to understand the hand-outs.

Most people find that when they get into the habit of putting all the details into hand-outs their presentations become leaner, sharper, and more focused on the audience. Audiences warm to the presenter more because they're not being asked to work hard during the presentation – they can relax and enjoy the message.

And, counter-intuitively, when people know that 'the facts' are written down on a piece of paper that they can double-check later, they tend to believe them more and challenge them less. Audiences are strange!

> **SIGNPOST**
>
> Make sure you're clear on the difference between slides and hand-outs. Ask yourself: 'Is this information essential *during* my presentation?' If not, put it in a hand-out.

Dealing with slide decks

'But what we do with the slide decks we've been given?' is a question I hear a lot. I also hear a lot of pain and frustration behind the question. People are really asking, 'How do we give a good presentation when the slide deck is so bad and/or limiting?'

First, remember the golden rule – the slides are not your presentation. They are a support for your presentation. Your presentation is your connection with the audience.

There's a lot of bad thinking around slide decks. Many companies create them because they want to standardise messages, guarantee quality, and control the outcome of presentations. They often get exactly the opposite result.

When presenters are given slide decks, it's easy for them to become lazy and restricted. They turn up to meetings, fire up the slides, and read through them. The underlying thinking is, 'The slides are the presentation, so if I go through them then I must have done the presentation.'

If you present like this, you're really just reading out a brochure. It might be a bit better than just emailing, because at least you can answer questions, but it's not ideal. Worse, the presenter is much more at the mercy of time and technical pressures because the slide deck leads the presenter, rather than the other way round.

The best approach to slide decks is to still follow the 'Busy Person's structure'. The fact that you've got some pre-planned and designed slides should not stop you from being clear on what your goal is, who your audience is, what your three main points are, and what your summary and punchline will be.

I also recommend that you do this work without looking at the slide deck, at least at first. You'll find that if you do this, when you do look at the slide deck you'll be much clearer on which parts of the deck are helping and which are hindering you.

Once you've written the structure on a piece of paper, then open the slide deck and go through the deck with the following questions in mind for each slide:

- If I were the audience, would I need this slide to understand and believe the main message?
- Is this slide serving my goals as a presenter?
- Is this slide really a hand-out, rather than a slide?
- Does this slide support my message or detract from it?
- Is it easy to understand this slide within a few seconds of looking at it?

While you're doing this, you'll notice a few things:

Some slides are just 'filler' but you'll need to keep them, especially if you're working for larger firms where the branding and structure is out of your hands. Introductory slides, placeholder slides, and farewell slides often fall into this category. They don't serve your goals, but neither do they do any harm, and you need to keep them.

Some slides support your goals and add credibility to your message. These are the ones to focus on during your real presentation.

Some slides detract from your goals. Where possible, remove these slides. They were probably created by someone who doesn't know your audience and doesn't understand that presenting is not about passing information via slides. If you can't remove them (often in larger firms, the slide deck is untouchable), then plan, practise and rehearse how you'll deal with them in front of your audience. Phrases such as, 'The next slide is really a hand-out, so I'll skip it for now,' work well. Make sure you've planned this in advance, though. It looks clumsy in real time if you have to read the slide yourself before deciding whether the audience needs to see it.

I worked with one client who realised that about two-thirds of the slide deck was irrelevant or boring to her next audience. So, right at the beginning of the presentation she said, 'I know that you want to get down to what really matters, so I'm going to skip through most of my slides today and focus on the top three. I'll leave all the slides as a hand-out at the end, and I'm happy to take questions as we go.' This is an elegant way to say, 'I've got to do the slide deck, but none of us need to suffer because of it.'

SIGNPOST

Run through a slide deck in advance, so that you know what you need and what you'll delete or skip during the presentation.

CHAPTER FIVE

The Not-so Busy Presenter

If you find you do have a bit more time to prepare, the advanced tips in this chapter will be invaluable for nailing that big presentation.

Presenting in teams

'So, who's starting?' I asked the four people standing near a laptop at the end of the room.

One of them looked at the laptop, clicked a slide, and looked at the first name.

'Oh, it's Leo,' she said.

That first moment told me everything I needed to know: although this team were one day away from presenting an extremely important presentation as a crucial part of their pitch process, they hadn't rehearsed their pitch – *not even once!*

I needed them to understand how important rehearsal is. 'Let's go to two minutes from the end of Leo's part,' I said.

There was the inevitable shuffling because Leo didn't have a clue what was supposed to happen two minutes from the end of his part of the presentation. I asked him to click through to his penultimate slide and start from there.

He mumbled a bit and then looked at Sarah, one of the team. 'Are you going to do the strategy part next?' he asked her.

'Oh, yes,' she said. She looked at Leo. She looked at the slides. She asked Leo for the clicker: 'Um, well, the strategy part of this project is important, as you'll see on the next slide.' She clicked through to the next slide. It read 'Implementation'.

I made them stop. They were intelligent people (all my clients are intelligent!) and they got the point quickly. When you're presenting in a team, the whole presentation has to work well – not just your part. In fact, if one part of the presentation is much better than the others, it can work against the overall presentation since the 'good' presenter will make the others look even worse than they already are.

All the basic work on the whole presentation still needs to follow the 'Busy Person's structure', but there are several things that you need to focus on specifically in a team presentation as opposed to an individual presentation:

TEAM GOALS AND ROLES

Do you have one overarching goal for the presentation? Does each member of the team understand this goal, and can they commit to it?

As with a single-person presentation, your team needs to do the work to identify the goal. I strongly recommend doing this work together, so that everyone is committed to the same goal. If you can't do that, then give the rest of the team a clear understanding of what the overall goal of the presentation is. If they don't know this, they can't structure and prepare properly.

MINI-GOALS

Does each presenter have a separate mini-goal? If so, do those goals complement the main goal, or do they contradict it?

A big advantage of a team presentation is that you get to build many moments of 'peaks and troughs'. It's appropriate in a team presentation to have mini-goals throughout, but the team still needs to know what the overall goal is and how each part fits into that goal. It's worth having this discussion before beginning work on slides or anything else. The other advantage of being clear about this is that it helps everyone to know whether or not they're just repeating what another team member has already said.

BEGINNINGS AND ENDING

Does the entire team know how each part of the presentation begins and ends – especially how the person before them will end their part? Do they know how the entire presentation begins and ends? In theatre terms, does everyone know their cue?

Rehearsal is obviously crucial here. In fact, rehearsal cures most team presentation problems. The key thing here is to get everyone together and, once you're sure that all the team members understand the overall goals and purpose of the presentation, to then have a quick run-through, focusing on the beginnings and endings of each person's presentation. You need to be sure that each part works well on its own but also that it contributes to the success of the overall presentation.

This is also the ideal time to be 'cruel to be kind'. Some people are naturally stronger at presenting than others. Some people will be strong on data but weak on 'performance', and others might be the opposite. Some might be naturally fast and energetic, some slower and more thoughtful.

There's no right or wrong here, but make sure that you use these strengths and weaknesses to the advantage of the entire presentation. Don't put people who are similar in presentation style next to each other, for example – vary the pace a bit. Make sure that your strongest presenters open and close the presentation, since they're the ones the audience is likely to remember most.

HAND-OVERS

One of the easiest ways to improve a team presentation is to rehearse the hand-over moments. Simply knowing what you have to say to introduce the next person, and knowing what your own cue is, will cut redundancies and keep your presentation energetic and flowing. It also makes you look more professional and prepared.

However, there's another tactic you can use here that will transform your team presentation from 'good' to 'great'. Instead of merely handing over from one presenter to another, you can ask each presenter to build a moment of interest, suspense, or intrigue for what's coming next. Compare these two examples:

JOHN: 'Ok, so that's my part about the technology itself. Now Jane is going to talk to you about your strategy over the next twelve months.'

JANE: 'Thanks, John. So, let's look at your strategy over the next twelve months…'

Written like that, it almost sounds like a parody, doesn't it? But this happens every day.

Look at how they could have done it:

JOHN: 'Ok, so that's the technology. As you can see, it's robust and, if implemented well, really will solve the needs you've got. But that leads us to some crucial questions – how do you implement it? When should you implement it? Should you do it in stages, or go all out? How have people reacted to different implementations in the past? Jane has some answers to these questions that I think you'll find fascinating.'

JANE: 'Thanks, John. So, yes, most people at this stage are excited about using this new technology but have lots of questions. I think it's really useful here to take a step back and look at a twelve-month strategy, starting with the question, "Where do you want this tech to take you in the next twelve months?"'

The second version is so much more interesting for the audience. You're creating a mini-narrative and leading the audience along a path of intrigue.

CHOREOGRAPHY

I don't mean that you need to dance! There is nevertheless an element of choreography to every team presentation. Are you all going to be standing? If so, how and where will you stand? Are you all going to be sitting? If so, do you know when to start moving from your seat to keep the energy of the presentation going? You won't be surprised to know that I'm going to recommend some rehearsal here.

Rehearsing presentation choreography prevents awkward pauses. When you rehearse, before each part make sure that the next person is ready and starts without a break in the flow. This is sometimes as simple as making sure that people are sitting in the correct order, or that they start moving just before they start speaking, to be in the right place at the right time.

I worked with a client once who transformed one

part of their presentation simply by speeding up the amount of time it took each team member to get into place. By making sure that each person was ready to start talking as soon as they were introduced, the team kept a sense of rhythm and flow in the presentation, and they never let the audience's attention drop.

QUESTIONS

Who is going to handle questions? Are you sharing them among the team? If so, is everyone aware of their role in this?

Usually, questions will come at, or near, the end of a presentation, so it's important to get this right. Questions are a great opportunity to cement the credibility that you've already created through your (obviously excellent) presentation.

To make questions go as smoothly as possible, make sure that you're playing to your team's strengths. Take some time before the presentation for everyone to predict the kinds of questions they'll be asked, and to decide which person will answer each question. You can also delegate 'types' of question. For example, 'Anne, can you cover any finance questions, and Mark, can you do any implementation questions?'

Lastly – and this is a technique I recommend a lot – make one of your team a 'question compere'. Their role is not to answer questions but to field them out to the appropriate person on the team. The person in this role needs to know the team well, of course, but also needs to be a good, credible presenter in their own right. Curiously, the audience begins to treat the question compere as being on their side – they treat them as an ally, which can build some useful bonding. The question compere also gets the chance to expand on audience questions in a way that further builds credibility and trust for the team.

TIMINGS

It sounds simple, but does each member of the team know how long their part should be?

The best way to get timings right is through rehearsal. You'll need to be tough about making everyone rehearse – you won't believe how resistant people are until you get them to try it!

It's a rookie mistake to assume that everyone will stick to their own timings without a rehearsal. Under the glare of an audience, even the shyest of people can go off on hour-long monologues, and the most extroverted team member can suddenly forget their part and go quiet after thirty seconds.

THE 'DIRECTOR'

Who is ultimately responsible for making this presentation work? If the presentation is important (and if it wasn't, you probably wouldn't be reading this), it's usually sensible to appoint one of the team to act as a 'director'. This is particularly true when the team is presenting to an external audience and the presentation needs to appear expert.

In theatre terms, a director's role is simple: they have to be the eyes and ears of the audience. For a team presentation, the role is the same – the director has to oversee the presentation and make sure that, from the audience's point of view, the presentation is fulfilling its own goals. This person should be given ultimate responsibility for making sure that the presentation works. Ideally, use an external expert since the director has to have the personal credibility and authority necessary to get people to act on their suggestions.

If you're using one of your own team as the director, make sure that their role is clear to everyone. Their job is to keep the team focused on the goal and on track in terms of time. A good director will also have a feel for when the ebb and flow of a presentation is right. They also need to be a diplomat, which brings me to the sticky point of...

EGOS IN TEAMS

The great advantage of a team presentation is that it's often interesting for an audience. We hear a variety of voices and a range of ideas. The downside is that teams are full of differing levels of competence and often full of competing egos.

The world being the way it is, of course, it's often the case that the worst presenter has the most clout on a team and wants the most 'stage time'. In many team presentations, there is nearly always a direct relationship between the amount of power a person has internally and the amount of time they are given in the presentation. Sometimes this can work, but it's not the most rational way to divide a team. You may also have to deal with someone who has their 'set' presentation and doesn't want to deviate from that, even in a new team presentation.

The best way to deal with most of these ego issues is to start with goals, right at the beginning of the presentation process. Stick to facts, rather than personalities, and every time there is a difference of opinion keep reminding people what the goals are, and ask them, 'What best serves the goal?'

It's worth reminding people right at the start of the process that the most senior people in the business are not necessarily the ones who need to make the most impact on an audience – especially if the audience is a potential client. Making this point *before* you start working on the presentation is much easier, because people are much less attached to their part of the presentation when they haven't got any material yet.

VISUALS

Someone needs to take responsibility for the 'look' of the presentation. The look of a presentation goes deeper than just the slides. Remember that your audiences make emotional, as well as rational, decisions about you. If you're going to give a team presentation where the outcome is important, then make sure that the director takes a step back and gives the presentation a visual once-over. Are all the hand-outs as attractive as they can be? Do the computers look good, or is one of the team bringing their exhausted old laptop, covered in badges and dents?

As far as dress code is concerned, no one needs to be a stylist on the team but you want to make sure that there are no horrible clashes – think in terms of having a 'tone palette'. My corporate colours are purple and grey, and whenever I present I make sure that I'm dressed in grey with a purple pocket square or tie so that I look prepared and consistent with my own slides.

Choreography is also important when thinking of visuals. The director should make sure that team members are not crossing each other in an untidy way when getting up to do their part of the presentation and that no one is distracting the audience, for example by rustling their papers when others are presenting or looking out of the window during a key message!

There's a lot of detail in this section, but if you follow all of these guidelines you'll find that you have a team presentation that is world class. There's another hidden benefit too: if your team is well rehearsed and prepared, and everyone knows exactly what they are doing, then they feel more confident, and they start working better as a whole team. That confidence and obvious ability to work together transmits itself to an audience.

SIGNPOST

- Make sure your team is rehearsed.
- Make sure that everyone knows their cue – how will they start and how will they hand over?
- Know how the team will deal with questions.
- Make sure that everything looks good.

Mind your language

'Broadly speaking, the short words are the best, and the old words best of all.'
Winston Churchill

Words can weave a spell that can change the world. Take the case of Martin Luther King – his creative, clear, and confident oratory created profound and powerful political change.

As presenters, we can learn a lot from the way that the world's best orators use language. They all use techniques known as 'rhetorical devices'. These are tools that you can use to enhance the power of your communication quickly. The most useful ones for business presenters are:

- Alliteration
- Assonance
- Repetition
- Lists
- Metaphor
- Contrast
- Simplicity

In 1910, Theodore Roosevelt delivered a speech in Paris at the Sorbonne. The speech is called 'Citizenship in a Republic', and a section of it has become world famous. Here's the first sentence of this section:

'It is not the critic who counts; not the man who points out how the strong man stumbled, or how the doer of deeds could have done them better.'

Roosevelt was a clever man, and he knew exactly what he was doing here. Let's break it down. First, read it out loud (yes, really!). Notice that it's not exactly 'natural' speech. It's clear that he's not just giving information, he's trying to create an effect. He's trying to engage the audience emotionally as well as intellectually. The language has a rhythm and is hypnotic. It's not accidental.

Read the first seven words aloud and notice the effect of the two 'C's of 'critic' and 'counts' – exaggerate them a bit and feel the effect this has. They're hard, crunchy sounds and are deliberately repeated. The sound itself reinforces the meaning that Roosevelt wants to get across.

Notice how many times he uses an 's' sound: in 'points', 'strong', and 'stumbled'. Say the whole sentence out loud again, this time emphasising the 's' sounds too, and notice the effect this has. Now read the rest of the sentence. I'll wait. Notice the 'd's?

This is all alliteration – the repetition of consonants – and it's used deliberately and to powerful effect. The sound of the language supports the meaning and lends weight and gravitas to what is being said.

Let's look at another rhetorical technique Roosevelt uses in the next part of his speech:

'The credit belongs to the man who is actually in the arena, whose face is marred by dust and sweat and blood; who strives valiantly; who errs, who comes up short again and again.'

In the first sentence, we get a repetition of the opening 'c' in 'credit', but Roosevelt is too good a speaker to use one device for too long, so he switches to assonance – the repetition of vowel sounds – in this case with repeated 'a' sounds: 'actually' and 'arena'.

Say this sentence aloud and see how it feels when you're *a*ware of the *a*ssonance. It helps to make his point much more resonant and more memorable. In this case, it worked so well that most Americans call this speech 'The Man in the Arena'. Roosevelt is also using simplicity – it's easy to understand this image.

Notice what comes next. It's a list, and it's a list of three: 'The dust and sweat and blood'. Most good speeches use lists, because it's easy for speakers to 'build' a list vocally. Try saying this list out loud, increasing the intensity from dust to sweat to blood, with 'dust' being weakest and 'blood' being strongest. Including lists and building the intensity of the lists is an excellent way to keep your audience's attention and add some suspense to your presentation.

Roosevelt has even more to teach us in this final section of his speech:

'… who knows great enthusiasms, the great devotions; who spends himself in a worthy cause; who at the best knows in the end the triumph of high achievement, and who at the worst, if he fails, at least fails while daring greatly, so that his place shall never be with those cold and timid souls who neither know victory nor defeat.'

Notice the repetition of 'who' – he uses the word four times in this single sentence. Try saying the sentence out loud, slightly emphasising the word 'who' each time. Repetition is a powerful means of making your message memorable.

Roosevelt is also using contrast – notice how 'best' is followed quickly by 'worst', and 'victory' by 'defeat'. At its strongest, this technique is known as chiasmus. Not just contrasting words but contrasting entire ideas or arguments: 'Ask not what your country can do for you, but what you can do for your country.'[7]

I hope that this section has helped you to become more sensitive to the possibilities of rhetorical devices. Remember that presenting in front of other people is not just about the information you give, it's about how you *affect* people with the information.

For crucial presentations, adding some heightened language will help you to engage your audience and increase the memorability of your message. Instead of 'Q4 update', you might talk about 'A strong strategy for success'. Instead of 'We need to change, and there isn't a lot of time to do it', you might try, 'Change is challenging, but it's essential that we embrace it early'.

Remember also that spoken language is very different to written language. What might look annoying and strange on paper can be powerful and affecting when spoken out loud. Conversely, what makes perfect sense on paper can sound boring and forgettable in live presenting.

You're now ready to go out and present using heightened, intense, powerful language. And if you need a reminder, just re-read the first sentence of this section!

---

7. John F. Kennedy inauguration speech, 20 January 1961, Washington, D.C.

SIGNPOST

Here's a short section of Helen Keller's tremendous speech 'Strike Against War'. See if you can spot how many rhetorical devices she uses that you can borrow for your next presentation:

'No, I will not disparage the editors. They are an overworked, misunderstood class. Let them remember, though, that if I cannot see the fire at the end of their cigarettes, neither can they thread a needle in the dark. All I ask, gentlemen, is a fair field and no favor. I have entered the fight against preparedness and against the economic system under which we live. It is to be a fight to the finish, and I ask no quarter.'[8]

The Big Client

This is the one. *The* client. You've spent ages getting the meeting, and you've pinned all your hopes on a successful outcome. You're nervous, the result really matters, and it's all hands on deck. If you win this pitch, all your money problems will disappear, your personal credibility will soar, and you'll be able to stride around your office godlike while lesser mortals look on in awe.

The good news is that in this book you've already learnt everything you need to know to deliver an

---

8. Helen Keller, 'Strike Against War' speech, Carnegie Hall, 5 January 1916.

excellent presentation. If you follow the structure and ideas that I've given you so far, you'll be on safe ground.

However, our brains are mischievous things – it's exactly when a really important presentation or pitch is coming up that we tend to get busy with other things, forget all the useful stuff we've learnt, and try to 'wing it' on the day.

Here's the first golden rule for The Big Client: The secret to success is entirely in the preparation.

This is not rocket science, but I've seen clients make the mistake over and over again of failing to spend enough time on the preparation for important presentations. I've known clients to spend more time thinking about the right jacket or shoes to wear to a client meeting than they spend on their rehearsal.

Magicians have their own version of Murphy's Law: 'Anything that can go wrong will go wrong, and it will always go wrong when it matters most.' With The Big Client, it's even more important that you are natural, relaxed, and spontaneous, but it's when you're most likely to be stressed and uncomfortable.

It's in your interest to make sure that you're prepared. And then a bit more prepared. And then ever-so-slightly-more prepared than that. It's counter-intuitive, but the more prepared you are the more spontaneous you will be because you'll feel more confident. The more confident you feel, the easier it is for you to be natural and relaxed.

Here's another counter-intuitive thing about presenting: The Big Client knows that they're a big client. They get pitched to all the time. They've seen the slick slides and the over-enthusiastic presenting styles. What they're not used to is an easy, relaxed presentation in a conversational, natural style that's focused on what matters to them. If you can deliver this kind of presentation, you'll be streets ahead. Don't skip the preparation!

The second golden rule here is: Know them and their problems better than they know themselves.

Every minute you spend getting to know as much about this client as possible will pay dividends in your pitch. Think particularly of their business challenges, priorities, and objectives. Are you pitching against an incumbent? If so, why? Is the incumbent bad, or is the client just trying to get them to work harder? Why are they looking to change? What's the cost of not changing?

And on a personal level – what kind of people are they? How do they think? How do they feel? What internal politics are really important for you to know about? Why are they giving up their precious time to meet you face to face? What do they *really* need from this presentation?

Don't worry if you can't answer all of these questions. You can always make educated guesses, and just having to think about what's going on in your client's world will make your presentation sharper. Basically, you've got two choices – you can either tailor your presentation to The Big Client's world or not. Always go with the first option.

The third golden rule for The Big Client is: the presentation is not as important to them as it is to you.

It's likely that, for you, this presentation will be

crucial. You'll have been thinking about it for days or weeks. You've run around gathering data and facing slides. You've asked for advice and comments. Ideally, you've practised, rehearsed, and rehearsed some more. On the day of The Big Client presentation you'll probably wake up (in a sweat) thinking about your presentation, and you'll keep thinking about it until it's over.

It's easy to forget that your client's perspective is probably profoundly different. They'll be busy with their own priorities and stresses. They'll have their own problems to deal with. Chances are that they look at their diary thirty minutes before you arrive and think, 'Right, I need to be in meeting room 3.4 for a supplier presentation. If it finishes on time, I can get this report finished'. That's it.

For you, the presentation is probably the most important thing on your agenda. For The Big Client it's almost certainly much lower on their list. If you remember this, it's much easier to be calmer and to match your client's energy levels. You're all adults who want the same thing – to solve a problem.

Online presentations

In an ideal world, all presentations would be face to face. However, in an ideal world, I'd also be living in Barcelona in the winter, be fluent in twenty-nine languages, and look good in selfies under any lighting conditions.

We don't live in such a world. Online presentations and teleconferences are here to stay – not because they're an effective way of engaging with people, but because they're easy, cheap, and convenient. Fifteen years ago, I had never given a single online presentation. Last year alone, I delivered twenty-seven and took part in many more.

Almost everyone treats online presentations as a means of delivering information, relying on slides to do this. This is an advantage for you – it's easy to stand out as a great online presenter if you're just a bit better than most.

Here are the guidelines:

Avoid online presentations where possible – particularly if you engage with clients. In my own business, I take great pains to try and see my clients face to face. It's surprising how often someone will agree if you suggest it. I have had many conversations where a client has suggested a conference call and I've said, 'We can do that, but I'll be in the area on that date, so why don't I come in and see you?' Even if some of the team have to dial in to the meeting, it's still a better presentation.

Tools. Online meeting technology is getting better all the time. Currently, I use Skype, Google Hangouts, Zoom, and GoToMeeting, although they might all be superseded by the time you read this. Where you have the choice, spend some time finding out what the most stable tool is – even the best presenter looks bad when the connection drops or slows down. If possible, connect physically to the internet with a cable. It's amazing how often a 'stable' Wi-Fi connection fails just at the moment you need it most. Also, make sure that all calendar invitations have the correct details and, where possible, that there are easy-to-click options for logging in to the meeting.

Voice. Invest in a decent microphone; don't rely on the one on your computer. Even a headphone jack mic is better than nothing. The better the microphone, the more authoritative and compelling you will sound. A pro tip is to put your microphone inside a box, with the open side of the box towards you – this will insulate the mic from background noise and make you sound like a true professional.

Visuals. If you're going to be on camera, make sure that there's nothing distracting in the background. Turn on your camera fifteen minutes before the meeting and check how you look. Make sure that you're looking into the camera lens, not at your own image on the screen, otherwise you'll look like you're avoiding eye contact. I draw a little smiley face on a post-it note and stick it next to the camera lens and talk to that.

Slides. Keep slides as simple and visual as possible. You'll lose people quickly if they have to read lots of information on the slides as you're speaking. Stick to strong images, screen grabs, and simple statements, or even single words if you can. I avoid video or complex animations as the risk of them going wrong is too high for me. I prefer to send the URLs so that people can watch those in their own time if they want to. Remember that you can always email more details, minutes, agendas, and hand-outs after the meeting.

Collaborate. One of the strengths of online tools is that they can encourage collaboration, and this helps to increase engagement. I often ask audience members to get involved, even if that just means clicking a thumbs-up icon to signify agreement. You can get people to type questions, fill in quick responses to opinions, and 'up-vote' or 'down-vote' ideas quickly. The more engaged your audience is, the more likely that you'll have a successful online presentation.

Emphasise the message. The major thing that you lose in online presentations is your physical presence. Strangely, this makes many people lean more on using slides and data. In fact, you should do exactly the opposite – focus more on the message, especially the hook. You should aim for as much clarity as possible. This often means having a straightforward agenda and being rigorous about any agreed outcomes.

Do as much offline as possible. Send agendas, suggestions, preparation materials, and questions to everyone in advance, and follow up with minutes and other information after the presentation. This makes the meeting more productive and cuts down on the amount of explaining you have to do. You can get straight to what matters.

Stick to time. If you start late or over-run you'll lose people's attention very quickly. Remember that questions are often delayed if people are typing, and that technological failures often cause time problems in the meeting. Budget for these in your preparation, and aim to finish at least ten minutes before the official time.

Even if you 'only' finish two minutes early, you'll have a better presentation. Most people react much better to a tightly-run agenda online than they do in person. Strict timings help to keep people's attention.

Create good habits. If you're presenting online a lot, encourage good habits such as punctuality, clear agendas, and collaboration. You'll get better at presenting online and your audiences will respect your presentations and meetings more.

Remember your competition. Your major competitor in online presentations is the wandering attention of your audience. Audiences get much more distracted when they're not physically in the room with you. Do everything you can to keep their attention. Dive straight in with a powerful hook, such as, 'Right, our department is going to have to justify a 21% cut, and this meeting is about whether we can do that. I'm going to start by showing you…'

If you follow the above guidelines, you'll have more effective online presentations and more engaged audiences, and you'll continue to build your reputation as an expert presenter.

How to ask for feedback

Don't wait until you're in front of an audience to get feedback on an important presentation. It's crucial to get the right kind of feedback before you deliver the presentation. The wrong kind of feedback is not only useless, it can also be damaging because you can be tempted to start making changes for their sake rather than because they help your goal.

A lot of people ask for vague feedback, and they just get vague answers:

PRESENTER: 'How was my presentation?'

AUDIENCE 'Oh, it was quite good. Maybe a little bit MEMBER: long near the end. I love your shoes, though.'

The best way to get good, clear, useful feedback is to give your colleague or friend who is acting as your rehearsal audience two bits of information:

- Who the real audience will be;
- What your goal is.

You can say to them, for example: 'I'd like you to watch this as if you were a very busy marketing director. You've already seen three presentations today, and you're a bit tired. My goal is to get you to a stage where you're interested enough in what I do to ask for a formal proposal.'

If you give your helper that kind of brief, you'll find that they're easily able to give you the kind of feedback that you need. They'll let you know when the pace is right for the kind of audience they're supposed to be, whether you kept them focused on the right things, and whether your presentation is likely to achieve the goal that you've set.

When presenting for feedback, resist the urge to explain yourself. Don't say anything that you wouldn't say to a real audience. Do your presentation *exactly* as you would in the real world. You'll get much better feedback this way.

It can be a good idea to wait until the end of your presentation before telling your colleague what your goal is. Ask them what they *thought* your goal was first, and you might be surprised (and educated) by what they say. You can then tell them what the actual goal is and ask them if you achieved it.

Remember that anyone who gives you feedback is doing you a favour, and respect that. Feedback is a time to listen, not to argue or disagree. Listen carefully to what your pretend audience tells you, even if what you're hearing is uncomfortable. Always remember to thank them for their time and effort, and offer to do the same for them at some point.

The only people qualified to judge the success of a presentation are your audience members. You are usually the worst judge of the quality of your own presenting, so listen carefully to anything an audience member says.

Ideal introductions

One of my main aims in writing this book is to encourage more people to present at an expert level more often. If you do this, you'll find that your credibility and influence grow. At a certain point, you may start being invited to present at larger events – at conferences, meetings, client events, and so on. It's a great privilege when this happens, and I recommend that you take every opportunity offered to you.

All of the advice offered in this book so far is

relevant to these larger presentations, but there is one extra thing I suggest that you do for them: write your own introduction and asked to be introduced.

Being introduced by someone else can build your credibility and get the audience on your side even before you've said a word. It adds a layer of professionalism and 'showbiz' to your presentation.

I take a written introduction to every presentation I give, and I always ask the host to read it exactly as I've written. If there's time, I ask them to quickly practise it with me since I want to avoid the possibility of a host 'winging it' or adding one of their own (never funny) jokes to my introduction.

When writing your introduction, think of 'CAR'. A good introduction will give you:

- **C**redibility (this tells the audience *why* they should listen to you);
- **A**nticipation (this gets the audience excited about listening to you);
- **R**elevance (this tells the audience that it's *worth* listening to you).

For example, an introduction could begin:

> 'Our speaker today has been Chief Marketing Officer at three household-name retail firms (credibility). During his time at ABC Ltd, he almost doubled their customer base and had record-breaking customer retention. Today, he is going to tell us how he did it without increasing his marketing spend (anticipation). Even better, he's going to show us how you can get buy-in from

your board to do something similar (relevance). I know you're going to learn a lot today, so please welcome... John Smith!'

I recommend that you keep your written introduction to this length or less. Don't make your host work hard – you just need enough to interest the audience.

I always put my name at the end, and always in capital letters – your name is the one thing that you definitely want the host to get right! Also, you'll find that if the host says your name at the end of the introduction you're more likely to get a round of applause, which sets the right tone. If your name is even slightly difficult to pronounce, rehearse it with the person introducing you. I print out at least two copies of my introduction, in 18-point font so that anyone can read it in any lighting conditions. I also email an advance copy.

It may seem strange that the last chapter in this book is about introductions, but it's deliberate. If you remember the structure of a good message, you'll realise why!

AFTERWORD

You've followed the MAP and have arrived at your destination – you now know everything a Busy Person needs to deliver a great presentation quickly, credibly, and confidently. But knowledge isn't enough – the real value of this book lies in how you start using it to become a better presenter.

There's an obvious way of getting better at anything: do it more often. But doing anything more often with bad habits will simply encourage a repetition of those bad habits. Grab any opportunity to present that you can, but make sure that you follow the guidelines in this book. If you do this, you'll build a strong and confident foundation and be well on your way to becoming an excellent presenter.

Think of the word 'presentation' in its broadest sense. A presentation can be a two-minute introduction to a meeting, it can be a project summary or update, it can be the launch of a new idea, or an announcement at an industry event. Take any chance you can to present yourself and your ideas to other people. Not only will your confidence and ability as a presenter improve – you'll also build your credibility, personal brand, and influence.

Work on one thing at a time. Choose one idea from this book that you particularly liked, or one area where you've identified a weakness in your presenting, and focus on that for a few weeks.

Ask for feedback often, and learn from it. Sometimes that feedback is formal, as in the previous section. Sometimes it's something you just overhear or a brief comment a few days after the event. Take feedback seriously and act on it where it's useful.

Video yourself. Where possible, record every presentation you give. Watching yourself on video is a great way to improve quickly and easily. You can buy a tripod for your phone cheaply, and just place it at the back of a room before you start presenting. Watch other presenters too – both good and bad. You can learn from watching anyone present.

Learn from other art forms. You can learn about presenting by watching films, listening to concerts, and reading novels. You can pick up great tips from comedians, magicians, and quiz show hosts. Try and understand how artists get their messages across. How do they hook your attention? How does a comedian get you laughing so quickly? How does a magician distract your attention? Look particularly at the structure of most forms of performance, and you'll notice that there are common themes – strong hooks, development in the middle, and always a clear punchline.

Set aside some time every few presentations to review what worked and what didn't. We're all busy people, and it's easy just to get on the treadmill with presenting. Even giving yourself fifteen minutes every few weeks to reflect on your presenting will pay for itself many times over. I've been presenting for a long time and I still make sure that at least once a month I sit down and review all the presentations I've given that month to see how I could improve. I may not be perfect now, but I'm a lot better than I was!

It's been a pleasure guiding you along the MAP process. I wish you every success on your continued presenting journey, and I hope that you come to enjoy presenting as much as I do. I'd love to know how you get on.

ACKNOWLEDGEMENTS

Everything I know about presenting I've learnt from others. I'm particularly grateful to my coaching clients and the many conference producers, event organisers, and business leaders who've invited me to speak at their events. I've never been able to believe my luck – they all paid me while I was learning.

I owe a huge debt of gratitude to James Harwood, who encouraged me to set up a business in 2010 and became the best business partner anyone could wish for. His wise, patient counsel, generosity, and humour have been an indispensable part of my own journey.

Many people contributed to this book without even realising it, through advice, support, encouragement, examples of excellence, gossip, theatre trips, and sometimes enough glasses of Rioja to keep the North Spanish economy afloat. By naming them, I'm sure to miss someone out (apologies in advance), but special thanks to Richard Cristofoli, Ray Yiu, Helen Rosemier, Richard Stemp, Catherine Philips, Karen Wentworth, Simon Bucknall, Mariano Trufo, Heidi Ashley, Myrna Atalla, William Buist, Alan Rae, Clare Josa, Kelly Molson, Simon George, Alex Bray, Lee Hathaway, Henri White, Paul Craven, Ian Rowland, Julie Holmes, Jez Rose, Ruth Polyblank, Daniel Priestley, Walter Fabeck, Ed Lamont, Saj Jetha, Matt Boardman and Paul Martin.

Huge thanks also to the eagle-eyed and talented team at Rethink Press – Lucy McCarraher, Joe Gregory, Verity Ridgman, and Maya Berger.

And, most importantly, and with love – Angela Warren and Alex Diaz, who are the reason I do everything I do.

THE AUTHOR

Lee Warren is a former professional magician, and a member of
the world-famous Magic Circle.
He has performed for members
of the Royal Family, celebrities,
and leading global brands, which
helped to balance the gigs he did
in hot, stuffy hotel ballrooms full
of terrifyingly drunk guests.

With composer Raymond Yiu, Lee wrote the sell-out
opera *The Original Chinese Conjuror* for the Aldeburgh
Festival. His libretto was described by the *Guardian* as
'witty and post-modern'. Lee trained as a performer
at the Academy of Live and Recorded Arts in South
London, and is a qualified teacher of the Alexander
Technique and a creative mentor for the Hospital
Club's Emerging Creatives Foundation.

A school report criticised Lee for 'speaking too much', but since 2010 he has been paid for it – as a professional presenter, keynote speaker, and presentation specialist. He has spoken in over twenty countries, and at hundreds of conferences and association events. He brings his performing skills and an irreverent, interactive style to business keynotes so that audiences 'laugh while they learn'. His key topics are presentations, sales, and networking.

Away from work, Lee is a biblioholic (one step up from a bibliophile), and is often to be found rummaging around secondhand book shops. Married to the world's loveliest Venezuelan, Lee is fluent in Spanish and very good at playing the piano badly.

SOCIAL MEDIA

[WEB] www.leewarrenspeaker.com

✉ lee@leewarrenspeaker.com

🐦 @leewarrenmagic